Learning Excha·

STILL *Screaming*

Birth parents compulsorily separated from their children

Lynn Charlton
Maureen Crank
Kinni Kansara
Carolyn Oliver

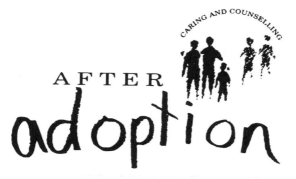

Published by
After Adoption
12–14 Chapel Street
Manchester
M3 7NN

© After Adoption 1998

Charity registration 1000888

**British Library Cataloguing in Publication
Data**
A catalogue record for this book is available
from the British Library

ISBN 1 953257 40 1

Project management by Shaila Shah, BAAF
Cover design by Andrew Haig
Cover illustration by Caroline Della Porta
Typeset by Avon Dataset Ltd, Bidford on Avon
Printed by Russell Press Ltd. (TU),
Nottingham

Acknowledgements

Parents Without Children

We are extremely grateful to the parents who worked with us, their personal experiences informed our practice and contributed greatly to the development of this service.

This project would not have been possible without the wisdom and guidance of Alison Dunne, Director, or the expertise of Catriona Morris who conducted the pilot study.

We wish to thank the trustees of the Henry Smith's Charity for funding this area of work and this book. We especially thank George Hepburn and Carol Meredith from the Tyne & Wear Foundation for administering our finances and for continual support and guidance; Jenny Biancardi for counselling supervision; the members of our development group; Barry Towers for his comments on graphics; Peter Selman and Kathy Mason from Newcastle University; and Maureen Crank for her drive and encouragement.

Finally special thanks to those who typed the manuscript; Lesley Croskell who wholeheartedly supported us and Geoff Turner at *After Adoption* who calmly sorted out our incompatible software.

Before Adoption

Grateful thanks goes out to all birth parents involved in the project for sharing their experiences and hopes, to Jenny Gomez for her contribution and support and Vera Martins for her ongoing support.

Thanks also to Sue Jackson for her joint leadership of the group and her support and help in working with the birth parents.

We would like to express our thanks to The Nuffield Foundation for funding the project throughout its two-year duration. We are very grateful for their interest and commitment to this work. We would also like to thank the Eleanor Rathbone Charitable

Trust for their financial support of this work.

Finally, special thanks to the Council of Management of *After Adoption* for their commitment to, and support for, the project.

Notes about the authors

Parents Without Children

Lynn Charlton is a social worker and trained counsellor. She has worked principally with children and families for local authorities and voluntary agencies. Lynn specialised in adoption work in 1988 and since then has gained considerable experience of working with all parties in adoption. She is an experienced trainer of professionals and carers. She presently works as a freelance counsellor, trainer and social work consultant.

Carolyn Oliver is an experienced social worker and has worked for a number of local authorities. She is currently working for a voluntary adoption agency. She has acted as advisor for local authorities developing policy and practice in fostering and adoption as well as child protection. She has been a member of a number of adoption panels and is currently Chair of one. She is an experienced trainer of professionals and carers.

Before Adoption

Kinni Kansara has a number of years' experience of working in community developments, within the refuge movement and in providing counselling to women survivors of physical, emotional and/or sexual violence. She was employed as the *Before Adoption* worker in the Summer/Autumn of 1994.

Maureen Crank is the Director and one of the founding members of *After Adoption*, Manchester. She is a qualified social worker and counsellor and has worked for many years in child care and mental health social work. She has specialised in family placement and has been a guardian *ad litem*. Maureen has also worked for a training company, scripting and editing training videos on social work issues. Since becoming Director of *After Adoption*, Maureen's interests have been in the developing of charities and the work of the voluntary sector. Maureen has personal experience of adoption.

Additional material was provided by Frances Coller and Sue Jackson.

Contents

Preface

This publication is derived from the work of two small, innovative projects, one in Durham and one in Manchester. The Durham project, *Parents Without Children*, was based in the Durham Diocesan Adoption Society and the *Before Adoption* project was based in *After Adoption*, Manchester.

The book is an account of the two projects and is presented by the workers of both; Lynn Charlton and Carolyn Oliver of *Parents Without Children* and Kinni Kansara of *Before Adoption* and Maureen Crank, Director of *After Adoption*. The book is being financed by Henry Smith's Charity, which funded the *Parents Without Children* project and want to see this valuable work disseminated as widely as possible. We wish to thank Murray Ryburn for providing the Foreword to the book, Hedi Argent for editing the text and to Shaila Shah, Head of Communications at British Agencies for Adoption and Fostering (BAAF) for managing the publication process on our behalf.

Both projects were carried out during a period of intense discussion about adoption practices, particularly openness, and latterly the reallocating of resources from child protection services into family support. The work of these two projects should help further this discussion; it also identifies a client group which is disenfranchised in many ways.

This group's experience of adoption seemed to be part of the 'permanency movement' of the early 1980s, which Joan Fratter says 'recalled the philosophy of rescue which had characterised the activities of the Victorian philanthropists'. The belief was that the welfare of a deprived child is best served by his or her being prevented from having contact with birth relatives. Parents were rarely allowed to continue to be a resource to their children after adoption and there is little evidence of a change in this.

The work of these projects shows how much we still have to do in relation to providing services before and after adoption for non-consenting parents.

Maureen Crank
Director
After Adoption

Foreword

The adoption of children against the wishes of their birth families represents the most forceful of interventions by the State into family life. This is so because, aside from death, only adoption or freeing for adoption extinguish absolutely and irrevocably all former parental responsibility. The parents of children who are adopted compulsorily become, in law, strangers to their children. They will never again be permitted to exercise a voice in the key decisions in their children's lives or be entitled, without a court order, which is very rarely granted, even the most basic exchange of contact with their child, such as the giving and receiving of a Christmas or birthday card.

The evidence indicates that there has been a steady increase in the proportion of adoptions involving the dispensation of parental consent. Thus contested adoption hearings constituted less than two per cent of all hearings in 1966 (Grey and Blundell, 1971) and this had risen very slightly to two per cent in 1972. However, in 1984 they reached 11 per cent (Fratter, 1996) and they have climbed ever since. In 1995, in figures supplied by the Lord Chancellor's Department, 30 per cent of all non-parent adoption orders and 57 per cent of all freeing orders were contested (personal communication, May 1997).

In the child welfare field there is no more disenfranchised group than these parents whose ties with their children have been permanently severed. There is also no better test of the worth of any profession than how it treats those who are least able to exercise a say in the services that they want and how they should be delivered. The legal mandate requiring local authorities to provide a service to meet the needs of birth parents is clear: Section 1 of the Adoption Act 1976 requires local authorities to provide services to the 'parents and guardians of such children' who 'have been or may be adopted'. This service is in particular to include 'counselling for persons with problems relating to adoption'. Both common sense and the small amount of available research (Ryburn, 1992; Mason and Selman, 1997) would lead us to the conclusion that adoption against parental wishes will cause problems for some, if not all of the parents concerned. However, as this book clearly establishes, drawing together as it does the experiences of two projects aiming specifically to serve such birth parents, unless the services that are offered are sensitively designed and tailored carefully to specific and unique requirements, the likelihood that they will be effective is probably remote.

In some respects the problems encountered by birth parents who lose their children compulsorily parallel those where there have been adoptions by relinquishment. In common with situations of relinquishment there may therefore be long lasting feelings of sadness and depression which may magnify with the passage of time. There may be a deep-seated yearning and a strongly perceived need to search which are also emotional components of unresolved bereavement by death. The loss of a child either compulsorily or by relinquishment may also lead to deep-seated feelings of guilt, centring particularly on a belief that more could have been done to have prevented the adoption. Birth parents of children adopted by relinquishment and those adopted compulsorily may also share feelings of anxiety about the welfare of their child, and an intense wish to know about a child's progress and development. Common too are pervasive anxieties about how the child who has been adopted will come, in time, to view his or her birth parents. Finally, parents in both non-consenting and relinquishing adoptions may report difficulties in the parenting of subsequent children and in their personal relationships.

Yet there are, it seems, and as these studies highlight, added dimensions of difficulty in coming to terms with adoption for birth parents in non-consenting situations. In particular there may be intensification of feelings of self reproach and recrimination compounded no doubt by the very public judgement of social failure that compulsory adoption brings. The parents of children adopted compulsorily face major hurdles in establishing or re-establishing a sense of self worth for they are all too aware of how little credence is likely to be attached to their views about why adoption occurred. They know, indeed, that their accounts are all too likely to be dismissed as stemming from nothing more than anger and hostility towards a system that found it necessary to remove their children and commonly, too, they express disabling fears that other or subsequent children may also be removed.

This book is of vital importance to social workers in the adoption field because it is the first and only study to offer an account of services specifically designed to meet the problems of the birth parents of children adopted compulsorily. The two projects described in this book represent significant developments in good social work practice and individually and collectively they demonstrate that it is possible to work effectively with some of social work's most alienated service users. But it is not easy, and crucial to the process of effective working, as the studies highlight, is the suspension of personal values and prejudices which would otherwise stand as barriers to the engagement of birth parents in a service which can meet their needs.

In particular the accounts of these two projects, one of which was based in Durham and the other in Manchester, underline the need for an independent service which is not associated in the minds of birth parents with the agency which took the decision to remove children from their care. The importance of the independence of such an agency has been highlighted in the past by the first independent post-adoption agency, the Post Adoption Centre in London. There is provision in the 1976 Adoption Act for local authorities, in meeting their statutory duties, to engage the services of voluntary agencies; pre and post-adoption support for contesting parents is an area where this is likely to be more beneficial than in any other.

Taken together these two studies offer us a measure of detail, which we have previously lacked, about the stages of grieving and bereavement for birth parents who lose their children through the courts. They offer guidance and practical help to professionals and policy makers working in this field, help to establish the parameters for a good and effective service and bring a measure of clarity concerning its necessary constituents. Ultimately the innovative work that has been undertaken in these two projects serves to remind us, in a child welfare world now driven by emphasis on risk, service plans and quality assurance, that in its origins social work began as a profession concerned to meet the individual and distinctive needs of those who are most isolated and socially dispossessed. This book offers us the clear message that a strong sense of commitment to such fundamental principles can still make a significant difference in the lives of vulnerable people.

Dr Murray Ryburn
Director of Social Work
University of Birmingham

References

Fratter J, *Adoption with Contact: Implications for policy and practice*, BAAF, 1996.

Grey E and Blunden R, *A Survey of Adoption in Great Britain*, HMSO, 1971.

Hughes B and Logan J, *Birth Parents: The Hidden Dimension*, Department of Social Policy and Social Work, University of Manchester, 1993.

Mason K and Selman P, 'Birth parents' experiences of contested adoption', *Adoption & Fostering*, 21:1, pp 21–29, 1997.

Ryburn M, 'Contested Adoption Proceedings', *Adoption & Fostering*, 16:4, pp 29–38, 1992.

A birth mother in prison

After Adoption was asked by the local authority concerned to undertake some work with a young woman who was in prison. She and her partner had been convicted of an offence which had led to the death of her child. The following is a brief account of that work, followed, with her permission, by extracts from some of her letters. I believe her letters speak for themselves and indicate the importance of undertaking this type of work, not just for the benefit of the birth parent in her own right, but ultimately also for the benefit of the children in their adoptive placement. Some factual details have been altered to preserve the woman's anonymity.

The young woman, whom I shall call Katie, was causing concern within the prison as she was self-harming. Her two surviving children had been made the subject of Care Orders following her offence. They were placed together in foster care and had been "freed" for adoption. Katie had recently attended this hearing but had spoken to no-one about her situation, despite having spent several months in prison being offered support from a number of sources. Katie's probation officer attempted to prepare the ground for my first visit, but apparently Katie faced the wall and although seeming to listen, made no response.

On my first visit to meet Katie, I initially did most of the talking. I explained that *After Adoption* is an independent organisation, a charity and one of our aims is to support birth parents whose children are adopted following care proceedings. I explained that, no matter what she had done, or what had driven her to do it, or what she hadn't done, she would always be the children's birth mother and nobody could ever alter that fact. I suggested there was still a role for her to play in the children's lives. I talked about working with other birth mothers and the sorts of things they had said to me. For example, how difficult it was knowing someone else was caring for your children and not you, feeding them, bathing them, watching them grow up.

Slowly, silent tears began to trickle down Katie's face and she began to give me fleeting eye contact. Eventually, she began to talk about how the emotion was so overwhelming that she knew inside she must begin to talk to somebody, or she would 'burst'. She talked about how she cut herself to create a physical pain, somehow embodying the emotional pain she felt inside. She talked about guilt and how unbearable it all was. She talked about the recent court proceedings and what the judge had said and how she had felt. At the end of this session, we agreed to meet on a weekly basis initially. There was a visible change in Katie's appearance; she appeared calmer and more responsive.

In subsequent sessions we talked about how Katie could still contribute to her children's well-being. They needed to know about her and her background and, perhaps most of all, would need some explanation about what had happened and why, and that she loved them and had loved their sister. Social services had agreed to an annual exchange of letters between Katie and the adoptive parents.

Katie began to write things down and to put information together for lifestory books for the children. She worked on these on her own between sessions. She began to talk to me about the offence she had committed and the events leading up to it. Her account was harrowing and I could begin to appreciate why she had been in such mental torment. Nevertheless, I felt privileged that she had been able to talk to me and subsequently her probation officer and the psychologist about these events. I helped Katie with the wording of her letters for the children and to understand that the adoptive parents would need to decide at what age to share these with the children.

A major issue which preoccupied Katie was the fact that the court had granted her a "final visit" whereby the children would be brought to the prison to say goodbye to her. Although Katie desperately wanted to take this last opportunity to see her children again, she did not know if she could handle it. We spent a lot of time preparing for this visit, working out who would be present, where it would take place, signals she could give if she needed "time out" or for the visit to be brought to a close and, most importantly, who would be available within the prison to support her that evening and at the weekend. The probation officer gave her full support and obtained the co-operation of the prison authorities, for example, Katie was allowed to visit the playroom where the visit would take place, beforehand.

The most difficult part of the "final visit" for Katie, and for me, was the waiting. Once the children arrived, she coped incredibly well. The older child recognised her and responded warmly to her; the younger one was less sure and tended initially to cling to the escort. Katie, for her part, was delighted to see the children and the progress they had made. They began to play happily with the toys, on the slide and with Katie, while I took lots of photographs. Afterwards, Katie cried bitterly and clung to me and her probation officer, but was proud of herself because she had managed to make the experience a positive one for her children and for herself.

In the sessions that followed, not surprisingly, Katie seemed depressed and once again withdrawn. She said little but would sit with me and cry. She was grieving for the loss of her children. The goal she had been working towards had been achieved and now there was an emptiness. Nevertheless, there was something more open and natural about the way she was grieving and she began to talk more about the death of her other child and other losses in her life and about her upbringing.

The anniversary of the child's death was approaching and weighed heavily upon her. Katie, of course, was unable to visit the grave. Although it was in another part of the country, through my contacts at *After Adoption* I was able to arrange for a sympathetic birth mother to visit the grave on Katie's behalf. She laid flowers, tended the grave and sent photographs for me to hand on to Katie.

Being incarcerated presented other difficulties for someone in Katie's position. There were the obvious difficulties of lack of privacy, restriction of freedom and being unable to cry or go for a walk when she felt she needed to. Katie developed coping techniques, such as going to the gym or playing sport. She also had to deal with the reaction of the other women, some of whom regarded women like Katie as the lowest of the low, and learning who one could and could not trust was important. Another low point for Katie was when a fellow prisoner, who had been very supportive, was released.

My involvement with Katie had reduced from meeting her weekly to fortnightly (as she began to utilise other forms of support available within the prison) and eventually to monthly. The children, by now, had been placed with prospective adopters. The adopters had received the lifestory books Katie had prepared and found them very moving. I understand that it helped them form a more positive and realistic view of the children's birth mother and influenced them in agreeing to meet Katie. Katie had felt, for some time, that she wanted to meet them; as with the "final visit" the prospect scared her, but it was something she felt she must do. Social services agreed to the meeting and a date was set. The social worker would transport the prospective adopters. A prison officer and I would be present and the probation officer on hand in the adjoining room, should Katie need "time out". Katie and I agreed to save our final three sessions – one for preparation, one for the visit itself and one for "tying up loose ends".

I am full of admiration for the way the prospective adopters and Katie handled the meeting. It was an extremely powerful experience for all concerned and took a great deal of courage on all sides. A lot of tears were shed and Katie rushed out of the room several times when things became too much for her. In retrospect we should have offered the same facility to the adopters. The couple talked frankly about themselves, how they had met and their marriage. They talked about the children, things they had said and done and how they, the adopters, already loved them. Although painful for Katie to experience, she needed to hear this. She had prepared a list of questions which the prison officer asked on her behalf. The couple gave Katie a beautifully framed compilation of photographs of the children which the prison authorities subsequently allowed her to keep, and Katie was able to say to them the things she had wanted to say. Photographs were taken of the birth mother and adoptive parents with their arms around each other, smiling, and all parties left with a positive view of each other and, perhaps most importantly, as *real* people. The adoptive parents promised to talk to the children about their birth mother and to help them establish contact, if they wished, when they grew up.

In my final session with Katie, she talked about how much more at ease she now felt, having met the adopters and knowing who was caring for her children. There was a feeling of immense relief. Although the feelings of loss and grief – for the child who died and for those who are adopted – are still there, Katie has, hopefully, learned to cope with them better and to realise that there is still a part for her to play in her children's lives, albeit a very different part from that of raising them herself.

Frances Coller

Letters from a birth mother in prison

Dear After Adoption

It was nice of you to come and see me on Friday, even though all I did was cry – but crying can say it all.

How I feel . . .
1. *Suicidal*
2. *Cannot cope*
3. *More depressed*
4. *Not being able to carry on*
5. *Knowing that my children are with other people. They are loving and caring and have responsibilities for my children. Doing the things that their mother should be doing for them.*
6. *Not knowing whether my son is all right and if he needs any more medical treatment*
7. *Feeling really low*
8. *Crawling back into my shell*
9. *Not being able to concentrate*
10. *Feels like all of my insides have left me to be with my children.*
11. *Wondering if I will ever see my children again, especially when they both get old enough to come looking if they do.*
12. *Feels as if I am growing weaker instead of growing stronger.*
13. *Thoughts about next month. Do not want the anniversary to come at all.*
14. *Wondering what will happen when I get out of here – whether it is safe or not.*

15. *My past is haunting me and I cannot get it out of my head.*
16. *Still not been able to come to terms with anything that has happened to me.*
17. *Suffering badly*
18. *Feel badly damaged on the inside*
19. *Nightmares are coming back to me because I am having sleepless nights again.*
20. *Wishing that I could have done things differently.*
21. *Feeling guilty*

Dear After Adoption

I really appreciate that you were there with me on the last visit with my children. That is something I will never forget about very easily.

Extract from a letter for a son's lifestory book

Son, I have nearly finished your scrap book and it is now 1997, and I am thinking about you and your brother all the time. Life is getting easier for me as I am coping with what happened and with other things like being in prison and getting used to the idea that there is someone else looking after you both.

Well, I hope that when you and your brother start to get older, you will both understand what has happened and why you are in another family. I hope that you can forgive me and that you know that I will always love you very much.

I am due to be released in 1999, and when I get out I will have to start a new life again. I do not know what the future may hold for me or you, but I hope that you are happy and that you are able to love your adoptive parents the way your adoptive parents love you. Who knows that one day we will meet up again. I will always love you son, and I will always be thinking about you both.

All the love in the world,

Your Birth Mum

Extract from a letter for a son's lifestory book

You were born on 15th of May 1994 at the hospital and you weighed 8lbs. You were and still are a beautiful baby boy, but now you are two years old and you are very big for your age now son. You have been through a hell of a lot.

You were badly injured when you were tiny and now you are older and are a bit better than when I saw you last. I was arrested on 4th of November 1994. That was the last time that I've seen you before I got sent to prison and if I had done the right thing at the time, you would be with me now at this very moment in time, instead of us being away from each other and being separated.

And it is difficult for me to accept you not being here with me, but I will have to accept it. Well, my darling son, I love you very much, more than words can ever say. I will write a bit more tomorrow night. I love you son and I am missing you very much. I will never stop thinking about you.

Dear After Adoption

I was happy to hear from you so soon, but it was a nice letter even though every time I think about it I cry so much that my eyes are sore from crying.

Dear After Adoption

I know prospective adopters have been found for my children and that my son is going to nursery and the children have met the adopters and they have gone to stay with them, so things are going well.

I am glad to hear that the prospective adopters would like to meet me. I think that is a great idea. I have always said that I would like to meet the adoptive parents so that it would be easier for me to meet them and to know who is looking after my children.

Dear Prospective Adopters

I just want to say thank you for coming up to see me. I realise that the visit was hard for you both, and if it was not for you I would not have had the opportunity to meet you both. I know what you were saying was right. I know that you will love and care for my children in the way children should be loved and cared for. I thought that you both were lovely people and knowing you has made me feel more confident that they will be okay and looked after and loved by two people who I have met and liked.

I know you will talk to them about me and you won't stop them from looking for me when they are ready. I also want to say a big thank you for the photographs that you brought up for me. They mean the world to me, especially as I know now that the children are in the best of hands and that they are really looked after by two amazing people who I have met and I will always have the picture of you in my mind.

If the children do come looking I will tell them about the visit from what I remember about it. You will have already told them about it, but I can talk about it too. I would just like to say when the children are grown up and they come to find me I would want them to keep in touch with you both because you are their parents now.

I have been allowed to keep the photos up. I have them in my bedroom and on the shelf beside my bed. I hope that you will keep in touch and exchange photos and letters each year through social services. I feel more settled now we have met and I am glad that we did it.

Dear After Adoption

I thought that I would write you a letter just to say that I am all right and I am thinking about you all the time, because you were involved with me for a long time and I just thought that I write you this letter.

I just want to say thank you for helping me through the difficult times and for building up my confidence about my children and other things. You have been marvellous while you were here with me and I want to thank you for being there for me at the adoption visit as well and for being so supportive.

I am all right in here. It is not too long for me to go now and I just wish that my children were with me when I get out of here, but that is impossible. I hope that they come back looking for me when they are 18 years old.

I am still working in the prison with my mates, and I just had an exam on Friday just gone, so we are waiting for our results.

This is just a short letter so I will sign off now. I hope that I hear from you soon.

With love

Introduction

The two pieces of work described in this book present a unique picture of a group of adults who have had little attention paid to their needs within the adoption process. The projects were different in that *Parents Without Children*, in Durham, was a larger project, with two white workers – one full-time, one half-time – and an administrator. *Before Adoption* in Manchester was smaller, with one part-time black worker.

This area of work is very hard to fund and sadly the *Parents without Children* project closed at the end of its three years. *Before Adoption* was a pilot project, funded for two years.

In drawing together these two similar yet different projects, it is important to look at the historical background and how they came about. *Parents Without Children* was founded following the Adoption Law Review in 1992.

The Review of Adoption Law began in 1990 with the publication of four discussion papers between 1990–92, which covered adoption practice and the implications for all parties involved in adoption. In the consultation paper in 1992, it was acknowledged that services should be provided for birth parents by social workers not involved in the adoption plan or by independent agencies. It was suggested that services needed to be made available to birth parents whether or not they agreed to the adoption of their child, and should continue post-adoption in recognition of the pain and grief associated with losing a child to adoption. It was accepted that if birth parents wished to be kept informed of their child's progress, once placed for adoption, then they ought also to be informed of any breakdown. There was a general recommendation that parents should be involved in the adoption process and that their wishes and views should be taken into account. These proposals, along with the recommendations of the other consultative papers, promoted an air of optimism about the changes in adoption legislation as far as birth parents are concerned.

It was at this point that *Parents Without Children*, funded by Henry Smith's Charities, began working in the North East of the country and then, one year later, *Before Adoption* funded by The Nuffield Foundation was set up.

Both projects offered independent support, advocacy and counselling to birth parents. The *Before Adoption* project only worked with birth parents prior to adoption. *Parents Without Children* offered a service both before and after adoption. Both projects had a similar value base and the aims were almost identical.

Unsurprisingly, common feelings were voiced by the users of both projects. They all highlight feelings of worthlessness, public humiliation and a wariness of services, particularly of social services. Common losses were identified in self-worth and confidence and the impact of these on health and relationships. These findings have been included in the research of Hughes and Logan (1993).

Birth parents felt that information used in court was either irrelevant or not checked out. This caused additional stress and there are good examples of this in both projects. The birth parents felt that they were in a no-win situation during assessment and knew before it started that they were not going to be allowed to keep their children.

It was usual that once the decision for adoption was made, the workers were reluctant to discuss the child with the birth parent and tended to guide the conversation towards other subjects. This added to the sense of powerlessness for the birth parents.

It was common for birth parents not to understand the adoption process. They also felt that they were often frozen out of plans for the child and that, if they were withholding their agreement, they were considered not to have anything to contribute to the planning.

In both projects an external group was set up, including birth parents, to act in an advisory/information giving role. The workers in both projects had independent supervision as well as management supervision and all the workers needed a high level of support. The advisory group and the workers both experienced deep isolation.

There were similar approaches to service delivery and in view of the difficulties birth parents have to obtain help, both projects included outreach work. There was a high incidence of cancelled and abortive visits and strategies to handle this had to be developed.

Having read and re-read drafts of this book many times, it is the feelings of the parents involved which stick in my mind. The title of the book was something we struggled with, until one day whilst talking to one of the workers on the new birth parent project here at *After Adoption*, I asked her for her first impression of the families she was working with. She had just returned from one of her first sessions at Styal Women's Prison. 'It's the scream,' she said, 'A silent one, but these women are still screaming.'

Maureen Crank
Director
After Adoption

References
Hughes B and Logan G, *Birth Parents: The hidden dimension*, University of Manchester, 1993.

PART 1 • PARENTS WITHOUT CHILDREN

Lynn Charlton and Carolyn Oliver

1 • Introduction

The documented experiences of relinquishing birth mothers in recent years (Tye, 1994; Hughes and Logan, 1993; Rendal, 1993; Post Adoption Centre, 1990; Winkler and Van Keppel, 1984) have highlighted the life-long impact of adoption and the resulting grief which was profound and often unacknowledged. Through the voice of the researcher and the influence of the Natural Parents' Support Group, we became more aware of their need for post-adoption services.

However, despite compulsory adoptions constituting a major proportion of adoptions handled by agencies today (Ryburn, 1994), the voice of those whose children are adopted against their wishes is rarely heard in the adoption arena. Whilst there are similarities in the psychological difficulties experienced by relinquishing and non-relinquishing parents, the perspective of those who do not relinquish is complicated by their disadvantage and marginalisation within state intervention. The sense of powerlessness experienced by these parents in the legal contest is underpinned by the loss of their children, and as a consequence of their disadvantage, few are able to represent themselves, let alone have a collective voice about their need for services, or influence social policy.

The Adoption Law Review in 1992 recognised that information and counselling services should be made available to all birth parents, recommending that:

'. . . *agencies should have a statutory duty to ensure parents of a child, whom it is proposed to place for adoption, are offered full opportunities to receive advice and counselling. This should be provided by a social worker who is not involved in the adoption plan if the birth parent so wishes.*' (para 28:6).

Additionally, the review advocated a role for independent counselling and advice to be made available (para 28:5).

The recommendations of this review set the scene for *Parents Without Children*, an innovative project which was set up to develop and provide services to birth parents which would not only meet their psychological needs but also enable parents to participate as active players in the adoption process.

We were able to develop client-led services in this area of work which represented the perspective of those parents who used our services, so that credence may be given to their voice in future adoption practice. This chapter outlines the development of *Parents Without Children* and the work that was achieved.

Context

Assessing the viability of a service

To assess the viability of such a service a pilot study was set up in 1992 with financial and practical assistance from Cleveland Social Services Department (SSD). Examining records over a three year period (1989–1992) a potential group of 147 birth parents was identified, who had had children compulsorily adopted in that period and who might wish to receive services if they were available. The pilot study conducted by a colleague, Catriona Morris, clearly identified a demand for post-adoption counselling services but also highlighted a wariness expressed by these birth parents of help offered to them. Many birth parents felt unworthy of help due to their sense of public humiliation at having fought and lost a legal battle to parent their children, and those who desperately wanted help did not want to seek support from the statutory agencies which had removed their children. They described feelings of anger, and feeling useless, forgotten, rejected and judged.

The findings of this study were the basis for seeking funding for an innovative piece of work which would initially be confined to the Cleveland area, and, if successful, be expanded to offer services in the North East region.

Parents without Children was set up in 1993 as part of an adoption agency in the voluntary sector, Durham Diocesan Family Welfare Council, a long-established adoption agency whose work responds to the lifelong needs of all parties in adoption and people experiencing fertility difficulties. The provision of a post-adoption mediation service within the agency had shown that those experiencing compulsory adoption had limited avenues available to them for help. In order to offer a comprehensive adoption service the agency began to consider provision of services to non-consenting birth parents as part of their post-placement work.

An independent grant allowed the project to be funded separately from other work in the agency, giving the freedom to shape the project in the course of its development to meet the demands of the client group. This was an important factor because within the first six months the project expanded to meet the demand by self-referring birth parents for a counselling support and information service earlier in the adoption process. This meant that parents contacted the project for help at different stages. In general, those contacting the project pre-adoption often did so directly after a court hearing (usually the granting of a Care Order), or around the time of termination of contact. Post-adoption, contact with the project was triggered either by a life event, e.g. their child's birthday, the birth of another child or becoming aware of the service.

Developing an operational structure

To some extent the funding determined the main components of the project; included in the funding was provision for research and evaluation. The project was unique and innovatory and therefore it was felt the findings should reach as wide an audience as possible.

The funding allowed for the appointment of one full-time and one part-time professional staff and a full-time administrative worker. Research and evaluation was commissioned from Peter Selman, Head of Social Policy, and Kath Mason at Newcastle University. The evaluation took place over a three year period (August 1993 – July 1996). Project staff were supported by a development group consisting of professionals with a wide range of experience. This group provided a forum for debates of relevant professional and practice issues as well as contributing to developmental strategies. The participation of birth parents grew as the project progressed with many parents becoming involved in training, evaluation, publicity and the overall direction of the programme.

Initial consultation was provided by the Post Adoption Centre, London. As the project developed, strong links were maintained with the Family Rights Group, London, and *After Adoption* in Manchester which subsequently set up a similar project. Counselling supervision was offered by an accredited supervisor outside the line management structure.

From the outset the project had three main aims:

- to provide counselling and support services to non-relinquishing birth parents;
- to research the impact of adoption on the lives of birth parents so that future services may be developed to meet their needs; and
- to disseminate our knowledge to as wide an audience as possible so that birth parents are given a voice in the adoption arena.

Setting up a project without a predetermined framework required us to think carefully about our value base, the operational structure and our approach to the services we were offering. We were concerned about some key points:

- how to maintain our independence;
- how our previous work experience in adoption would affect our work with birth parents; and
- how to find an approach that would empower parents to seek out and use the service.

Many new projects spend time team building and identifying ways to meet their objectives having generally accepted the philosophy of their organisation, but often little time is spent discussing beliefs and personal or professional values to establish a shared value base. We considered this to be a crucial task as we were very aware that our work would entail representing a group of birth parents whose views are not often heard and, indeed, are frequently discounted.

Understanding what influences one's own professional practice is an important part of one's ability to have empathy with another. We wanted to be responsive to the perspectives of birth parents and this required exploring our own biases, assumptions, beliefs and pre-judices, in short, suspending our judgement or preconceptions of situations we faced. This was not an easy task as we were both aware that our views about birth parents would be influenced by our past experience as childcare and adoption social workers. The importance of clarifying our value base to create an opportunity for openness, and therefore empathy, can be illustrated by an initial visit to Mary, a birth mother requesting post-adoption counselling.

Talking about a situation which occurred prior to the removal of her three-year-old son, she recalled the violent relationship she had had with her partner whom she described as having extreme mood swings. Following a severe assault resulting in her receiving serious injuries, she described sitting alone on the sofa downstairs, while her son lay upstairs in his urine soaked coat, screaming for comfort, protection and physical care. She told me he had been there for some time, was hungry and frightened, but that she was unable to move or attend to him. She talked graphically about feeling guilty about not responding to him but how, at the same time, she could not bear the physical or emotional closeness of another human being because she felt so hurt, rejected and demoralised. Her emotional numbness prevented her from responding to her child.

On hearing this story it struck us that had we been wearing our "social work hats" we would not have been able to hear or understand her perspective. What we might have been likely to perceive was a mother who was unable to care for or protect her child, someone who neglected her child's welfare for the sake of her own needs. Child protection would have been the primary concern and placing the welfare needs of the child as paramount, we would have found the evidence to support the view that the child may be neglected or at risk.

We are not suggesting that this child was not at risk or that social workers should not seek to intervene in cases where they believe children may be at risk, but this case highlights how one's perception of a situation is formed by preconceived ideas, assumptions, expectations and the role we are playing.

Whilst it is impossible to suspend all prejudices and assumptions (Spinelli, 1989), the attempt proved to be an invaluable process, allowing us to hear and accept birth parents' experiences while simultaneously establishing a firm foundation for the project, independent from statutory roles.

It was from this process that we were able to identify our philosophy with clarity.

Philosophy

Our philosophy was based on five basic beliefs:

1. Birth parents are parents for life even if they are prevented from parenting their children.
2. Birth parents have the right to be well represented and supported

when there are legal conflicts to determine their children's future.
3. Adoption may be necessary for some children.
4. Adopted children have the right to form a true identity.
5. Birth parents have a role to play in their children's future and therefore openness should be mediated along a continuum; flexibility is needed to allow a child to feel secure in his or her adoptive placement but also to have access to information about his or her birth family's lifetime development, either directly or through a third party.

Deciding on an approach

We sought to find an approach that would enable us to learn from the client group whilst providing services to meet their needs. We recognised that parents who lose children through compulsory adoption previously received services from statutory agencies whose professional approach is firmly rooted in problem-orientated intervention.

Social work assessments are often carried out on what is immediately observable and measurable, with the result that service users may be perceived as one-dimensional characters. The quest of social workers to find observable methods of assessing risk, heavily promoted since the child abuse tragedies and enquiries of the 1980s, serves to alienate parents and families from their support systems. Literature (Ryburn, 1993) and experiences related by parents, reveals this is a dehumanising process which discourages respect for the individual, discounts the psychological effects of loss and trauma, promotes inequality and disadvantage, and results in humiliation and stigmatisation.

Developing an independent service created an opportunity to move away from traditional social work approaches and to develop a model which concerned itself with birth parents' accounts of their experience rather than the "objective realities of their case". Furthermore, we were in a position to address the issue of power differentials which so often exist between those providing and those receiving a service. This is important as birth parents commonly reported feeling disempowered by the services they had previously received.

Our approach required that we were accountable to the birth parents we worked with in that we demonstrated respect for the reality of their experience and remained open to whatever emerged. This was essential if the service was to be of therapeutic value.

These initial considerations directed us towards a phenomenological basis to the counselling model we employed, allowing us to engage in a parallel process to gain a body of knowledge that informed our practice.

The key differences between independent workers in this project and statutory workers are:

- project workers do not have a prior relationship with service users;
- they are independent from a statutory framework and therefore are free to work with the birth parent as their primary client;
- they have no prior knowledge of the circumstances of the service user other than that which the service user chooses to share during the initial discussion;
- on making contact with birth parents, project workers have no pre-set agenda and are not restrained by agency tasks; and
- the focus of any intervention is to empower birth parents to make informed choices.

Making the service available to birth parents

Our aim was that birth parents could access the service for themselves. Our carefully designed publicity leaflet included a self-referral form that could be returned directly to the project office. To further ensure a confidential service to parents, stamped addressed envelopes were provided; if social workers or other professionals made initial enquiries on their clients' behalf, parents could return the leaflet directly in order to access the service. This enabled parents to think carefully about seeking independent support when they required it and also emphasised our independence from statutory agencies.

Leaflets were displayed in public places and sent out to known non-relinquishing parents by supportive local authorities that agreed to make parents aware of the service. Knowledge of the project amongst professionals and community groups was thus quickly established.

Third party referrals were accepted but only if they were made in the full knowledge and with the consent of the birth parent. To maintain client confidentiality minimal details were taken from the referring agency such as name, address, whether pre- or post-adoption, whether the birth parent wished us to make contact with them and the legal status of the children involved. We had some difficulty in insisting that we did not require full details of "the case" from professionals who, we are sure, thought this to be odd practice. We sought minimal details out of respect for those seeking a service and, more importantly, to maintain our openness to the parents' perception of what had happened to them. It also helped to maintain our independence not to receive information about parents or the local authority's perspective of a case. This ensured that we did not in any way become part of the statutory decision-making process and any future clarification of decision-making could be done with the consent and on behalf of the parents with whom we worked.

Who responded

Birth parents came from a wide geographical area in the North East of England spanning seven local authorities (all adoption agencies), namely, Cleveland, Durham, Sunderland, Newcastle, Gateshead, South Tyneside and North Tyneside. Initially we targeted publicity about the project in one local authority area with a view to target-ing other areas as the project developed. The response was greater than anticpated with enquiries coming from across the North East region. In the period August 1993 to the end of January 1996, the project received 103 enquiries about services; out of these 65 parents chose to have an active involvement with the project.

The majority of referrals were from individuals, both birth mothers (75 per cent) and birth fathers (12 per cent), the remaining 13 per cent presented as couples.

Those who contacted the project during the process of losing children stated at the point of referral that they needed information about adoption procedures; this was given as the principal reason for seeking support. Following initial contacts with all birth parents, whether pre- or post-adoption, there was a general need for information, explanation of legal orders and terms, and knowledge of their rights, as they tried to make sense of their experience.

Outreach

The pilot study had indicated that this group would be difficult to reach and that their past experiences led them to be wary of help and support offered to them; many said that they would find it hard to seek out potential help for themselves and demonstrated a great need to check out workers.

For this reason we decided that a major component of our work would be making home visits or seeing parents at an agreed address or venue of their choosing. This allowed for the birth parent to take whatever measures they felt necessary to feel safe and to be in control of initial contacts. Often family members or friends were present during the first visit. It required patience, flexibility and time to allow parents to establish their trust.

In the early stages it also entailed a high incidence of abortive visits or rearranged appointments. With experience we attributed this to be equivalent to testing out if we meant what we said i.e. that we were offering them a service for which they would need to take some degree of responsibility. We also took into account that many parents led chaotic lifestyles in which they had to struggle daily with poverty, housing difficulties and parenting subsequent children in a context of fear of intervention by the authorities.

The problems in engaging birth parents were overcome as our experience grew. We learned that we particularly needed to acknowledge to parents that they might find it difficult at first to keep regular appointments, taking care about when and what time of day we made appointments as well as agreeing in the early stages what we should do if we found a visit to be abortive. The attention to detail in contracting with birth parents was in itself an empowering process and allowed parents to voice their worries and fears as well as clarify the position they were starting from.

In recognition that poverty and disadvantage are features of this group, we were keen to make the service accessible and yet at low cost to our users in terms of both money and resources. The outreach approach had further advantages, as it also meant the service was available to children remaining in their families, and enabled us to work with couples where new partnerships had been formed.

Outreach enabled us to respond within people's ethnic, religious and cultural contexts. Our limited resources and the fact that we were two white workers prevented us from offering services specifically directed at different minority ethnic groups and we worked in an area with a very small black British population. Nevertheless, we ensured that the birth parents of other ethnic groups with whom we worked had access to community resources and, on occasion, an Asian worker. Similarly we made our services responsive to disability needs, for example, using the local interpretation service for the deaf.

Consumer involvement of birth parents in the project

As our relationship with birth parents grew, many became very interested in *Parents Without Children* as a service. It was a source of support to many birth parents to realise that they were not alone in their situation and that we were aware of others experiencing similar pain and misunderstanding. It was important that the service was both client led and that a number of birth parents participated in the training and dissemination parts of the work. For birth parents whose own personal situation had left them feeling disempowered, the opportunity to give wider meaning to their experience was very affirming. We increasingly included birth parents in all aspects of our work. This was sometimes through involvement in the production of audio and video material for training purposes and also in writing contributions for articles and reports to our funders.

Parents also participated willingly in the evaluation of the project (Mason and Selman, 1996), sharing their personal experiences freely to promote understanding of the impact of adoption.

This evaluation by outside researchers identified both the pain of birth parents and the urgent need for the provision of independent services on a national basis. As project workers, we feel that it is also very important to present our personal journey in establishing a unique project that set us alongside birth parents; witnessing something of their experience and endeavouring to develop a model of service that recognised their voice.

2 • Birth parents' perspectives of compulsory adoption

The parallel development of client-led services in conjunction with the aim to learn more about birth parents' experiences and the impact of adoption on their lives, provided the opportunity to record the accounts of 65 birth parents. In doing so we have been able to identify common themes which highlight the psychological impact of compulsory adoption and the powerlessness birth parents feel during this process. We became quickly aware that compulsory adoption involves not only loss of children, but also a loss of self worth and confidence. The impact on health and relationships was compounded by that of the legal process itself.

Experience of the court process

Parents Without Children worked exclusively with contesting birth parents, both pre and post- adoption. Not surprisingly therefore, we learned a great deal about the impact of the adversarial process in general and court processes in particular. Adversarial processes exacerbate the original trauma and consequently birth parents are from the outset ill-equipped to participate. In addition it is clear that support mechanisms are either not available or denied.

Many birth parents talked at length and in detail about attending court as a traumatic experience which resulted in feelings of humiliation and a sense of betrayal by the local authority which had previously been perceived as a helping agency.

One birth parent, Leslie, felt the evidence given by the Social services department was stacked against her, and even as she re-counted the details of their evidence she seemed shocked and dazed. In her first session she repeated these details several times whilst crying. She felt discredited as a parent in court because it was proved that she was unworthy. She was too distressed to go back into court after being publicly humiliated. She was shocked that the social services department had presented certain facts as evidence.

In many of our sessions with birth parents they agonised over what was cited against them in court. They felt "raped" by the exposure of private family affairs – the microscopic attention to detail without putting it in the context of events in their life. They often felt information was used which was irrelevant. For example, evidence about inadequate provision of food caused great distress to Leslie. She repeatedly talked about how she had fed her children at her father's house because of her partner's violence. It was therefore true that there was no food in her house but for her the implication that she did not feed her children was very wounding.

Jenny described the horror of hearing evidence that she had fed her child "dog food". She later remembered that this was how her child referred to hot dogs. She had no opportunity to explain this and was subjected to the full force of the accusation in court.

Many birth parents who contacted us spoke of the way they saw facts about their everyday lives presented negatively.

We thought they were trying to help when all the time they were just watching for anything we did wrong.

One couple talked angrily of the involvement of a family aide. They described how she spent most of the day at their house, arriving before breakfast and leaving late at night. The husband resented her questioning his movements. She asked why he was eating his meal alone in the kitchen rather than with the family. He retorted that he wasn't going to have a stranger watching him eat his tea. They also described how difficult it was to relate to their children while being watched. One family aide they had had purely observed the care of the baby and ignored their little boy. A second had at least "mucked in". She had read stories to the little lad and also let them go to the shop on their own – they felt more relaxed with her. The first aide had given a bad report on them:

. . . she was only looking for the bad things. She didn't care about us. .

Alan described how the family support worker criticised him in her report for having the children in the kitchen while he was cooking. Alan was extremely angry about this as he had them with him because he wanted to be responsible, and he felt that having the children in the kitchen with him was safer than leaving them on their own in the other room.

We heard bitter complaints, over and over again, that the focus of court was only to judge whether the children needed to be removed from their parents and consequently everything was presented in that framework. This, of course, is the essence of focusing on the 'best interests of the child' which is the role of statutory services. However, the parents touched on a wider issue to do with the nature of our adversarial legal system, which, as Ryburn (1993) points out, is reductionist, divorcing individuals from their wider social and family context. It is not surprising that many parents felt their own needs for help and support were not being recognised.

Parents felt unable to prevent what was happening in court and despaired because they had sensed that everything had already been decided. Further humiliation was caused for some by a public portrayal of their own childhood experiences in care. They felt it was unfair and primarily used as defamation of their character rather than being relevant to the welfare of their own children.

The devastating impact of the courtroom is intensified by the isolation and lack of support felt by birth parents. Both Leslie and Helen spoke angrily about the fact that they had friends ready to support them, but they were not allowed in the courtroom as they were not party to the proceedings.

For birth parents in a state of shock and confusion, the efforts made to attend court hearings, both practical and emotional, are not adequately recognised. George described in detail the struggle he had to overcome financial difficulties to get to the court in a strange town. His determination to 'not give up on his children' enabled him to battle with his agoraphobia. He finally reached the court, fearful and exhausted. After the Freeing Order was made he became upset, but he was aware that even his solicitor was embarrassed and unable to offer him support.

Barbara voiced the frustrations of many when she commented that:

It's just a job for the solicitors but it's my life.

Birth parents felt that their solicitors deserted them by sending other colleagues. They looked to their solicitors for a more personal advocacy and were often dismayed to find that solicitors were 'playing a game'. Family Rights Group (1994) and Ryburn (1994) quote similar findings. The recommendations from the Family Rights Group are that family members should be entitled to have a friend / supporter at the court hearings. Many birth parents lost faith in their solicitors and changed them in panic at the time of key hearings. We were aware that birth parents had little understanding of the legal process and their choice of solicitor was often ill-informed and frequently based on their knowledge of a solicitor from very different "briefs".

Reactions to the isolation and impact of the court process could be severe and sometimes led to attempted suicide following proceedings. This was associated with an overwhelming sense of unworthiness, which also inhibited parenting of subsequent children.

Leslie described how she felt that she had nothing to live for and had tried to kill herself. She talked of 'not being any good' after the court evidence and how she was unable to parent her second child because she felt 'worthless' and publicly condemned.

Suicidal feelings often recurred at later stages of the legal process or when memories of it were triggered. Occasions that challenged self-worth frequently revived feelings of humiliation and despair. The shame of attempted suicide affected later situations as was clear in

Helen's case. Helen had taken an overdose following care proceedings but she did not discuss this or her experience of court in any of the counselling sessions; she just maintained a profound fear of returning to court over a contact issue with another child. She felt humiliated and wanted to avoid further exposure.

The loss of parental status and the common loss of partners at the same time combine to lead to a high risk of suicide following court hearings.

It became clear from all the birth parents who contacted us that court proceedings had a huge impact on their self-worth and self-esteem. Many felt betrayed by social workers who had been perceived as helpers and suddenly became opponents in the legal battle. This shift from one of enabler and partner to adversary was the most difficult for birth parents to take in and contributed to their anger towards the social worker.

The adoption process

The negative effect of the court experience is compounded by the confusion and lack of understanding about the adoption process itself. Parents were uncertain about the legal stages, terminology and their rights. This confusion was evident in the initial sessions and a dominating theme when significant court cases were imminent.

In the post-adoption cases there was ignorance about how the child came to be adopted in the first instance or a lack of clarity about the adoptive status of the child.

Ann did not know if her child had been adopted. She felt confused as to whether the child could have been adopted without her consent – muddled about different legal stages of the Care Order and Freeing Order – humiliated that she didn't 'know the words'. Many shared this confusion which may have been attributable to the lack of involvement in the adoption process or the emotional trauma experienced by birth parents which produces a psychic numbing referred to by Wells (1993). It became clear that the adoption process was running parallel to the anger, trauma and grief associated with enforced change. Birth parents are desperate to understand what is happening, to know the legal process and to understand their rights. Given the emotional crisis caused by the removal of their children, parents often fail to assimilate information at the time it is given. Therefore, it is not only a question of giving clear information but also of the emotional context in which birth parents hear it. Lack of attention to the timing adds to the obstacles for birth parents. Clarity of written information is crucial because the legislative process, particularly 'Freeing', is difficult to understand alongside primal feelings of fighting for one's child.

The gravity of a Care Order, generally after a lengthy period of interim orders and visits by guardians *ad litem*, is often accompanied by the first realisation that this is part of a plan to place their children for adoption and to stop all contact. Many parents grasp that they will still share parental responsibility after a Care Order but do not understand that the power to determine the extent of this lies with the local authority. Decisions are likely to have already been made about the child's need for permanent placement. By the time of a Freeing hearing, an adoption placement may already have been identified; in some cases the child may already be placed or settled with prospective adopters. This precipitates decisions by the court to endorse the plans that have already been made and acted upon in the best interests of the child. The disparity between local authority planning and the perception and rights of birth parent is often acute. Parents who are still actively engaged in a fight for their child are confused by Freeing as a part of the legal process. For Ann (mentioned previously) it was the dispensation of her parental consent in the granting of a Freeing Order which accounted for her not knowing if the Adoption Order had been made.

Birth parents usually regarded Freeing as part of the fight to retain their children, not the first stage in the granting of an Adoption Order. Any recognition by birth parents that their children's needs might best be met by others, was buried beneath the desperate fight to oppose the total loss of their parental rights. Smart and Young (Ryburn, 1994) highlight the contrast between the view that at a Freeing hearing 'the contest is usually all over bar the tears' and the birth parents' decision to contest. Many birth parents told us of their determination 'not to give up on their children' but were aware of their own confusion about the legal process in which they were engaged.

Further complications arise from misunderstanding the irrevocable nature of adoption. Birth parents expressed confusion about their rights post-adoption, particularly where contact was reinstated or continued.

Lack of involvement

Feelings of having been excluded from plans for their children were common and reflect the nature of the adversarial process. Whilst the birth parent is attempting to comprehend the seriousness of the court order and cope with bitter disappointment at their change of legal status in relation to their child, the local authority is working to prepare and secure the child's legal position towards adoption. The birth parents' suspicions that adoptive parents have been identified long before the Care Order was granted, is possibly correct. On application for a Care Order the local authority is required to present a care plan for the child; it is unlikely that they would say whether adoptive parents have been identified at this stage, unless requested to do so by the court. It is important to know that under the Children Act 1989 (Section 33.3), the granting of a Care Order means that parents and local authority share parental responsibility for the child, though the court may grant the power to the local authority to carry out the care plan (including adoption) and terminate contact with the birth parent (Section 34). Birth parents, however, have the right to be kept informed and to be involved in planning for their child.

Rose described how any attempts she made to obtain information about her children post-Care Order and pre-Freeing Application was met with the response that she needed to 'let go' and accept that the plan was adoption. The social worker clearly thought it was not 'therapeutic' to involve the birth parent at this stage. Another parent, George, remains unclear about the sudden change from allowing him contact visits in the foster home to terminating them in line with a plan for adoption. He commented:

> *I don't understand why they let me do all that visiting. It did my head in and it was all for nothing!*

Parents had a feeling of being 'closed out' of the adoption process. Helen felt that she had not been kept informed about plans for adoption since the Care Order. She was unclear about why contact would be terminated so quickly after the Care Order was granted. She recalled an explanation by the child's social worker:

> *Sharon needs a fresh start . . . severance of links between Sharon and her family are necessary to give Sharon this.*

Rose felt that the adoptive parents were identified long before she ever went to court and that there was some degree of collusion going on:

> *I know I'm supposed to have shared parental responsibility but it is like I've been pushed out. No-one seems to realise that I am still supposed to be involved legally. I am still a parent and yet the only person who has shared information with me about my child is the adoption worker. Sharon's social worker has frozen me out.*

It is interesting to note that Helen also differentiated between information given to her by the adoption social worker and the messages and lack of information given by the child's social worker. There may be valid reason for this, as the child's worker is primarily concerned with the welfare of the child at this stage and is probably in an adversarial position in relation to the birth parent. Surely this would support the recommendation of the Adoption Law Review (1992 Section 28.6) for an independent social worker to work with the birth parent during the adoption process.

Despite individual circumstances and experiences, all the birth parents said that they did not understand the complexities of the adoption process. Once adversarial court cases are in process, it seems that the notion of partnership and shared planning in the interests of the child becomes a nonsense because there is no shared perception of what is in the best interests of the child.

This is illustrated by Mary who was looking forward to a contact visit from her son. Mary was careful to liaise properly with her son's carers. A few weeks prior to the proposed visit she received a brief letter from Social Services saying the visit had been cancelled as there was a court case pending. The appeal referred to had not been brought by Mary and yet she received no explanation. She was very concerned about her son's response but the department refused to give her any information while the matter was in court.

Consent

The question of consent nearly always produced strong emotion. With pre-adoption cases it was an immediate issue, with post-adoption cases it arose when parents tried to piece their story together. Despite differences in legal stages there was a common feeling of having been pressed into giving consent, often on the advice of solicitors and social workers. For example, Mary felt forced to give consent after her partner, with whom she was no longer living, had given his freely. She consulted a solicitor but recalled being told 'the best thing you could do would be to sign as you have no case to fight for your children'. Reluctantly she gave consent but said that she didn't feel she had received adequate advice. At the time she felt very confused. Also, in the case of Cath, consent was given reluctantly on the advice of her solicitor who indicated to her that the contest for her children was over.

Helen had been persuaded by social workers to sign her consent to adoption, a course supported by her solicitor who presented this as a way of coming to accept the adoption of her child. Helen said that she felt pressed by social workers 'to make it easier for everyone'. She added:

> *I don't want to sign them because in years to come Sharon may feel I've given her away. I don't want Sharon's social worker and (family members) to say that I should sign so that Sharon can feel that I like the family she is going to. It is not about that. I know that Sharon's adoption will happen anyway whether I sign or not and her adoptive family seem really nice, caring, warm, but I couldn't live with myself if I signed the papers. I want Sharon to know that I didn't want her to be adopted.*

Many birth parents were like Leslie, unclear how the adoption of their children could have proceeded without their consent. One could assume this was due to not understanding the power of the court to dispense with consent either at the Freeing stage or under Section 16 (2) of the Adoption Act 1976.

The initial reactions to questions about consent were anger and protest which may be linked to underlying grief. Bowlby (1980) refers to the pain of grieving in terms of reproach and anger. Where the pain associated with grieving is perceived as an unjust punishment, the anger and blame are directed towards anyone who may have contributed to the loss which, in these cases, is usually the social worker who removed the child, or more usually social services in general. The idea of consent raised an overwhelming desire in parents not to give up on their children and not to betray them.

This is demonstrated by Alan who did not even discuss the issue of giving consent as his case was heavily contested.

> *I'm fighting for my kids. I'll take it to the European Court of Human Rights . . . I'll work hard and get the money together. I'll do everything, anything. I've never given up on my children and I never will. I'll just go on fighting — being there.*

Pamela describes how she

fought all along the line right up to the High Court in London. I wasn't going to give up even if it took everything I had – I would have gone to the European Court. But what could I do in the end? My solicitor told me not to break down and get emotional in court and then the Judge asked me how I would feel if my son came back now that two years had passed and got all upset because he wanted to go back to the mother he knew. It was then I knew I couldn't do anything more. I couldn't do that to my son so I agreed but it tore me apart inside. I felt like I'd given up but what could I do? I felt like screaming 'but I'm his mother'!!

Many birth parents like Pamela also felt self-doubt and a sense of betrayal. They felt that they were not worthy of their children and yet to consent to their adoption was rejecting them. This was a dilemma that caused recurrent pain even years later. Helen talked of feeling torn between wanting to acknowledge the new proposed adoptive parents as carers for her child's future, but also wanting her child to know that she was not given away and that fundamentally she did not agree with the severance of the blood ties.

Helen's account shows the unreasonableness of seeking consent from parents who basically do not agree with the adoption of their children. Consent is usually sought at a late stage when adoption is almost a *fait accompli*; the battle to secure the child's future by adoption has been essentially won, but for the birth parent the issue of having fought and lost remains. In these circumstances, being asked for consent seems to provoke primal instincts to protect the blood tie and the child from irreversible rejection or abandonment.

If the plan for adoption is opposed by the parent, an informed choice not to consent is their right and would seem both ethical and reasonable. The legal requirement to determine the question of reasonableness within the context of adoption law is determined by what is in 'the best interests of the child'. When perceptions about this differ, a parent who is opposed to adoption is measured against the 'hypothetical reasonable parent' (Lawson p 46 in Ryburn, 1994). If adoption is deemed to be in the best interest of the child then the parent is perceived to be unreasonable in withholding consent. Whilst the Review of Adoption Law (DoH, 1992) recommends non-fault based grounds for dispensing with parental consent (endorsed in the draft Adoption Bill, 1996), this merely serves the purpose of proceeding with the adoption on the grounds that it is in the child's best interest. Therefore little attention is likely to be paid to those who disagree. The "stakes" in contested adoptions are high. Birth parents find it hard to come to terms with giving up a child in a "no win" situation. The life-long guilt described by those we have worked with and other parents contacting the project, intensifies their loss and provokes a sense of unworthiness. In the words of one parent:

What kind of mother am I? I fought and lost and then gave in — I signed my children away. How do you live with that?'

There is a further complication when subsequent children are in the parent's care at the time of the adoption. How can you live with caring for some of your children at home unless you have contested to the end the adoption of your first child? A signature on a consent form actually says very little about the parent's views of the adoption application, or their circumstances.

One couple, Jim and Eva, had a third child and struggled with all kinds of explanations about the loss of their older children to adoption. Jim talked of having to keep fighting:

[If not,] *how can I live with my little girl at home?*

It became clear as we listened to so many birth parents having to face what they saw as the betrayal of giving consent in adversarial proceedings that this had grave implications for future direct or indirect contact, and consequently the possibility for birth parents to be a resource for their children would be lost.

The prevalent notion that it is unreasonable not to sign a consent when it is clearly in the child's best interests also affects the attitude of the adoptive parents towards the birth parent. In the training and preparation of adoptive parents it is extremely important that attention is paid to consent from the birth parent's perspective. There is a tendency to view a consenting birth parent as more worthy, acceptable and deserving more "sympathy" than a contesting birth parent. This can have far-reaching implications for adoptive parents' willingness to acknowledge the child's past and exchange information or consider contact.

Post-adoption contact

Many birth parents who contacted the project had their children adopted at a time when social work practice did not acknowledge the benefits of post-adoption contact and adoptions were largely "closed" adoptions.

All birth parents reported a desperate desire to know how their children were. Many "tracked" their children's lives by watching other children of the same age. One birth mother walked round the shops in order to become familiar with current interests, toys, books and fashions appropriate to her children's ages. A number thought that they had "seen" their children but were frightened to approach them. Some birth mothers reported that they knew where their children were but would not disrupt them.

All the parents celebrated their child's birthday – some buying birthday cards and displaying them. One mother whose son was removed at two years of age and is now 15, still buys a card, puts it up and sings "Happy Birthday". Such rituals helped parents who had no information to mark the passage of time. It frightened them that time was passing and they were missing their child's life. On the other hand, they longed for the child to reach 18 as they felt this was their only hope of learning about him or her. They hoped that their children would come looking for them.

A number of birth parents had other children at home with them. These children also expressed a strong desire to know about the lives of their brothers and sisters. William was very keen to be involved in making a video to be forwarded to adopted siblings about whom he had heard nothing for about twelve years.

Those birth parents who received some information and photos were immensely grateful and treasure even the smallest snippet of news. If there was anything to suggest that the child "took after" them they were thrilled.

The move from closed adoptions to allow at least an exchange of information has, in the UK, been greatly influenced by the voice of birth parents and adult adoptees and also by practice in New Zealand (Mullender, 1990). Like in New Zealand, Australia and the USA, consumer groups in the UK have advocated for more openness. Openness can be defined as 'a general approach to adoption which is not secretive and whereby as much information is transmitted between interested parties as can be, without detriment to the child'. (Adcock, Kaniuck and White, 1993).

The extent to which adoptions are now more open, and the form of this openness, cannot be understood without reference to the current legislative framework in this country. Decisions about adoption and contact usually follow adversarial child care proceedings. Adoption Orders, however, cancel out all previous orders and give adoptive parents full legal authority.

Changes in child care law under the Children Act 1989 have listed adoption as family proceedings and give power to the court to make Section 8 (private law) contact orders in adoption cases. As adoption cancels out any previous orders these technically need to be made after the Adoption Order is made. Courts are reluctant to attach Contact Orders to adoption unless the adoptive parents are in agreement, as it could potentially undermine their parental responsibility granted under the Adoption Order. Contact Orders are, in any case, difficult to enforce and lack of agreement or the need for outside enforcement call into question the whole purpose of a Contact Order.

Practice is developing to consider non-statutory contact arrangements between all parties, and several birth parents we worked with had had some form of post-adoption contact. The majority of contact arrangements, however, had to be negotiated through the same social services departments which were responsible for the contested adoption plans.

This raises important questions. How far can a social worker who is bound up in a contested adoption give a fair picture of a birth parent, when knowledge of this parent is based on collected evidence which focuses on failings attributed to the birth parent? How far are the fantasies of the adoptive parents about the birth parent fuelled by the perceptions of social workers who invariably would have been the targets of the birth parents' hostility and anger? Many of the birth parents we spoke to feared a negative portrayal of themselves was or would be given by workers to the adoptive parents.

For Helen, the attitude of the child care social worker towards contact post-adoption was evident at the time of the care proceedings. She recalls being told that open adoption was not for her and that she had no rights to ask about her child. Later she learned that the adoptive parents were willing to consider an annual exchange of information. This raised her hopes of being able to talk directly to the adoptive parents about her child's identity and her wish 'to reassure the adoptive parents'. She then learned that they were not prepared to meet her and she struggled not to be angry. She wanted to like them because they represented her child's future. She felt very concerned that:

It could be that they've been told bad things.

Helen's concerns were shared by other birth parents. A number felt betrayed and abandoned by the social worker. They spoke of 'being dropped, no longer important'. They expected the social worker to provide links with, and information about, their children, despite their own anger towards the workers. As one birth mother said:

She's got my kids now, she's not interested in me any more.

Burnell (1993) suggested that the relationship 'has become contaminated by the adversarial approach taken by local authorities towards birth parents . . . and the belief that the courts require termination of contact as a precondition for adoption'. He emphasised that the success of post-adoption contact or openness depends on co-operation between all parties, and advocated a mediation service similar to those in divorce situations.

During later stages of the project we received calls from guardians *ad litem* who were concerned about pre-emptive termination of contact before adoption. This also raises questions about the *timing* of decisions regarding the future value of post-adoption contact for the child: often informal agreements for contact are made when the legal contest is not concluded, and therefore the birth parent may not fully appreciate or feel able to discuss post-adoption contact. Views expressed by Tony were evidence of this. Tony only made minor reference to the agreed post-adoption arrangements for an annual exchange of information. He talked more frequently of trying to gain contact through the courts, despite being aware that he had no legal rights.

Ryburn stated that 'the realism of openness may still fundamentally depend on practitioners' (1990). Certainly from our experience of working across seven local authorities, this was apparent. For the birth parents who had some form of post-adoption contact, the attitudes of social workers were significant factors in how far this contact was prearranged and achieved. Birthdays are of such importance to birth parents that if, for example, they are promised a photo annually on a birthday, that is when they desperately need it. Delay or gaps in receiving information about a child's well being caused anxiety and psychological difficulties for parents. Often information was not received at the time or in the way that birth parents understood it to have been promised.

June commented:

I was promised some photographs but never got any. I haven't got any recent ones, only old ones but Julie won't look like that any more.

She had made contact with social services post-adoption and asked about photographs but feels she did not get a very good reception. The promise of photographs never materialised despite letters written to the local authority on her behalf by *Parents Without Children*.

We were told of instances when birth parents were distressed by what can only be described as insensitivity. One parent received a photograph of her children taken by the social worker on the day of the adoption with an accompanying letter saying 'the children are looking very happy now that it is all over'.

Jane had received no information about her son, now aged nine, since he was adopted as a baby. *Parents Without Children* wrote on her behalf to the placing agency. A letter from the adoptive parents was received but small pieces of information about her son were scattered among other comments like, 'he regards us as his real family' and 'he has made great progress since becoming a member of our family.' It seemed that the worker thought of this letter as a bonus with which the birth parent should be satisfied and not ask for more.

A number of agencies did respond positively to requests for information and contacted adoptive families when there had been no previous arrangements to do so. Even where the response was positive however, there were difficulties.

Cath described vividly her reaction to renewed contact after a period of 10 years. Contact was re-established with her children following the breakdown of their placement in their late teens. Cath says she cannot express her range of feelings about her children's adoption or about the contact now. She still thinks of the toddlers she lost and so it 'doesn't make sense'.

It feels like the children should be much younger. My memories are frozen in time. I lost two young children — two teenagers returned. Sometimes I look at them and think these aren't the children I lost, they are teenagers with thoughts of their own.

Parkes (1972) described pathological mourning and how the searcher carries the lost object in their mind; if the object or person is identified then anxiety diminishes. However, when the picture does not fit, the implication is that anxiety will continue. This was illustrated by Cath's confusion and comments about the toddlers she lost and the teenagers that returned. Her anxiety set in train a number of grief reactions: guilt, self-reproach and alarm resulting in her restlessness and anger directed at the unsatisfactory relationship between herself and her adopted children as well as the biological father. Cath now feels frustration and a sense of desperation. She felt responsible for her children's adoption but now finds it difficult hearing them blame her for it.

This is so hard to hear, I did search for them. I was the one to search, not their father.

Cath also feared she was not worthy of a relationship with her children and this was now getting in the way. She felt like not having contact with one of her children, as this child was not forthcoming about his own feelings. Her relationship with the other child was more open because this child freely expressed anger at being adopted. Cath even considered severing contact because it was 'too difficult' and 'too confusing'.

Cath had been helped by the local authority to re-establish contact: in the first place by registering her interest and later by approaching the adoptive families on her behalf. The views and wishes of her adopted children were clearly taken into account alongside a commitment on behalf of the placing agency and later a second agency, which handled the breakdown of the children's adoptive placements.

Janice requested photographs of her baby who was removed at birth. This placing agency was also supportive, and the adopters willingly provided photos of "their" son, now a teenager, at different ages. Janice, however, found that she couldn't cope with the photos all at once as she had to "grow up" with her baby. Time had to be spent with each photograph from babyhood upwards. It was clear that Janice was still traumatised by the loss and that the lack of information in the intervening years had not helped her recover in any way.

To a lesser degree these reactions were shared by other birth parents when they received photographs of their children. Their experiences demonstrate the need for post-adoption support services for contesting birth parents and highlight difficulties that arise when knowledge of, or contact with, their children is disrupted and not consistent. Perhaps this points to the importance of keeping birth parents involved throughout the planning stages for adoption, if post-adoption contact is to be meaningful and successful for the child. Co-operation between birth parent and adoptive parent is crucial. Therefore agencies or professionals need to be sensitive about the damaging effect of their attitudes or the delay in facilitating good relationships between the two sets of parents. We became acutely aware that birth parents are a potential resource for their children throughout their lives even when no direct contact takes place. Our experience suggests that if this is acknowledged, birth parents are very child-centred and imaginative in providing information for their children. Life story and video work outside the context of the adversarial proceedings can be therapeutic for the birth parent and the child, as well as valuable and informative for the adoptive family.

George, who was extremely angry with the social services department, was beginning to accept that his children would grow up with other parents. He desperately wanted information to reassure him that they were all right. Negotiations about an information exchange resulted in outbursts against his social worker and a consequent decision by the department to curtail information. George did, however, have the potential to be a resource and to support the placement. When he received information about his daughter's ballet classes he got some books about ballet from the library so that he could understand more about her interest and write better letters. He wanted his children to know that he had taken an interest in their new life. George also made several videos for his children in which he explained to them his sorrow and regret that they had not been given the family life he had wanted for them. He talked about himself and his wife pulling in different ways and the stresses and lack of good parenting that followed. He talked of his pain at losing them but also of his hopes that they were happy.

More attention needs to be paid in the early stages of placement as how best to engage both birth and adoptive parents to help their children to know who they are and where they come from.

Effects on health

The trauma of having a child removed through a contested adoption can have significant and long-term health implications. Many parents reported health problems which could be directly related to mourning their loss.

Most commonly reported were physical symptoms consistent with bereavement and trauma theories. These were principally sleeping difficulties, weight loss, poor appetite and vivid dreams. Dreams appeared to have two distinct themes: flashbacks about the removal of the child or dreams about searching and retrieval in which the child was restored to them. Characteristically, flashbacks are a symptom of post-traumatic stress (Thompson, 1989) whereas dreams associated with searching or retrieval direct attention towards finding the lost person. Parkes (1972) showed that the lost person can be recovered through dreams. However, in his study he found that within happy dreams respondents indicated that all was not well (p 81). This is consistent with the accounts of the birth parents in the project who also reported that on waking they became agitated to find that all was not how it had been in the dream. It would seem dreams are a form of problem solving, but as Parkes points out 'the problem of bereavement' is not solved as real recovery of the lost person cannot be achieved. This results in a 'sad awakening' (p 83).

Dreams and nightmares reported by Helen featured a searching theme. She had fears and anxieties about a recurring dream where she found Sharon as an adult with a baby face. She described having a good feeling about the whereabouts of the child – naming a specific town. Rose has repeated nightmares every time she approaches her own birthday – her child was removed on her eighteenth birthday. Sandra described a recurring dream in which her children are in the path of a combine harvester. In the dream she finds herself screaming and trying to reach them but a wall prevents her getting to them. The only information Sandra has about her children's placement is that they were placed on a farm.

Restlessness associated with searching had different manifestations. Many birth parents constantly looked at other children in the hope that they might be theirs. Lynda, Ken and several others reported great anxiety when children's deaths or accidents were reported on television.

I need to know that my child is all right. Is she dead or alive? If anything happens, would I get to know?

Searching was linked with desire for reunion.

During Sandra's contact with the project she claimed to have had a reunion with one of her children. Her wish for this was so strong that sometimes fantasy and reality became merged. She talked about her daughter in great detail and it was significant that she described her daughter's appearance, personality and behaviour as just like her own at that age.

Moving house was an issue for birth parents. Some had a great need to stay in the same house where they had lived with their children, so that they could keep a home to which their children could return. Others made frequent moves to avoid painful memories, and were driven by chronic restlessness and searching. Sometimes a sense of hopelessness resulted in apathy, ambivalence and an inability to hold on to housing. Once the first move had been made more usually followed. One birth mother moved three times while she was with the project – her moves, however, were all within a mile of the house from where her child had been removed and where the neighbours always knew her address.

For Leslie, the thought of moving from her home where her child had last lived with her triggered anxiety. She had a strong need to exactly maintain the environment most closely linked with her child. According to Parkes (1972) this is behaviour associated with patho-logical grief. Gorer (1965) referred to this need to preserve the environment as mummification, which he cites as a characteristic of chronic mourning. Leslie prominently displayed photographs and "unconsciously" bought presents and clothes for her lost child; this too is characteristic of the searching behaviour described by Parkes and the mummification described by Gorer. Dave said his mother had a cupboard full of clothes ready for his daughter when she came back.

The need to retain the lost child is graphically illustrated by Pauline's account of needing to keep her child's bedroom, which was located at the top of the stairs, complete with the door ajar so that she maintained a sense of her child. Despite pleas by her new partner to close the door she felt unable to do so.

I needed to keep this bedroom as it was for about four years after the court case.

In a more extreme case the child's bedroom was still intact ten years later.

Rose and her partner's situation was extreme. Their property had been badly vandalised when new neighbours learned about the removal of the children. For a while they lived in an upstairs room. When they were able to start re-decorating, we saw a room as yet completely bare except for one small wall which was painted and had flowers and a large photograph of the missing children. In a stark room it was a powerful shrine.

Unresolved grief affected Debbie in a different way. She was angry with parents who lost children through death.

They've got a grave to go to. I've got nothing and don't know where my child is . . .

She was angry that her grief was unseen and unacknowledged. After the Care Order she reported that she felt flat and switched off:

I was left feeling flat and worthless — but I do have something to offer them.

Debbie talked of her hopelessness and whole range of feelings:

Sometimes I feel guilty about what happened, sometimes sad, sometimes hurt.

She felt guilty about wanting to get the adoption process out of the way because it wore her out, so that she could 'begin to put some sort of order in my head'.

Debbie's feelings were echoed by other parents in the project; it is known that parents who have relinquished babies in the past are also left with a sense that their loss is denied by society at large. The result can be 'psychic numbing' which Wells (1993) suggested is perpetuated by secrecy in adoption. Isolation and helplessness was experienced by all the parents.

Bowlby (1980) referred to pining which is associated with feelings of despair, powerlessness and diminished self-esteem. Parkes (1972) noted that following bereavement individuals are sensitive to the attitudes and expectations of others. Writing about stigma Goffman (1963) found that lack of social feedback can result in the stigmatised individual becoming isolated, depressed, suspicious, anxious, hostile and bewildered (p 24). McCann and Pearlman (1990) commented that unsupportive or blaming responses from others are likely to contribute negatively to an individual's reaction to trauma. Given the public humiliation of being proved "unfit" to parent their children, it is not surprising that birth parents felt isolated or stigmatised.

The times when birth parents feel their loss most intensely are frequently times when others are preoccupied with jollity and festivity like at Christmas or New Year . Their misery is not publicly acknowledged in the way that it would be if they were bereaved. They are more likely to be told that they are unreasonable to wallow in their misery and that they should try and pull themselves together.

Not surprisingly birth parents worried about their mental health and emotional state – sometimes thinking they were going mad, sometimes at the mercy of mood swings, or showing irritability, misery, and unprovoked outbursts of anger that did not fit the immediate circumstances.

George said:

I'm like a pressure cooker, about to explode. It's doing my head in.

He suffered from panic attacks and agoraphobia.

Alan described feeling anxious and agitated. He had problems with sleeping and serious loss of appetite. He was treated for depression by his GP, but felt that tablets were not the answer and wanted someone to recognise his despair. He talked of vivid dreams, depression and incidents of self-harm or destructiveness triggered by anniversaries: Christmas, the children's birthdays and termination of contact. Periods of suicidal thought featured throughout the duration of counselling:

I can't live with this anger or bitterness, it's destroying me.

Lynda, a post-adoption birth parent, reported gynaecological and kidney problems, excessive weight loss due to eating and sleeping difficulties, along with an over dependency on nicotine. Whilst Raphael (1983) with reference to Bartrop (*et al*, 1977) commented on the likelihood of an increase in psychosomatic disorders following trauma, it would seem that the physical symptoms described by Lynda may well have been related to her prolonged and unresolved mourning. Parkes (1972) attributed physiological manifestations to a high state of arousal, linked to searching behaviour. This would perhaps explain the frequency with which Lynda referred to physical problems while she displayed signs of emotional restlessness and talked about a long-term need to search for her child.

Cath also spoke of sleep loss and confusion. She felt a desperate need to contact her children and to know about them. She talked about crying on occasion because she was not in touch with them. The crying did not stop over the years. She had a great longing to find them.

Sandra has had many years of ill health – she had been admitted to hospital for several exploratory abdominal operations but no physical cause of her illness was traced. Sandra also had gynaecological problems; she had several miscarriages and lengthy phantom pregnancies. During our course of work with her she became convinced that she was pregnant once again. She expressed extreme ambivalence – she was desperate to parent but terrified to have another baby lest it was taken from her.

Carol felt similar panic about pregnancy – quite justified as subsequent children were removed at birth. More recently her pregnancy resulted in an early miscarriage followed by later pregnancy tests which proved negative.

Two women reported pain and muscular problems which they 'knew' were because their own children were in pain. One woman hurt her leg crossing the road and later had confirmed reports that her separated son had been hurt at the same time. Her experience is consistent with the findings of other studies noted in the discussion of literature.

There are strong links (Bouchier *et al*, 1991; Hughes and Logan, 1993; Millen and Roll, 1985) between the grief felt by those who relinquished children in the past and these birth parents who were non-relinquishing. In addition to the lifelong mourning common to all, it would seem that contesting parents bear a sense of powerlessness and the stigma of losing children through the court process. This appears to have compounded their difficulties in being able to live with their grief.

Whilst it is not possible to account for other variables which may have contributed to how these parents deal with their loss, it is interesting to note that many raised issues in counselling about background factors, which they felt were affecting their ability to cope. Disruption in parent-child relationships during their early lives either through death, placement for adoption, abandonment or rejection by the mother were not unusual features. Research suggests that stress depends on how an individual perceives his or her loss or transitions following loss, on personality factors and cognitive style (Hodgkinson and Stuart, 1991; McCann and Pearlman, 1990; Parkes, 1972).

George returned in counselling to themes of abandonment and rejection by his own mother. He was at times a small boy feeling hurt, fear and anger. He was able to work on these layers of loss and to place the adoption in a context that felt important to him.

Horowitz (*et al*, 1980) suggested that a major factor in pathological grief is the activation of earlier self-images and role relationship models. In cases where conflictual relationships are evoked and identified, this has a negative effect on the grieving process. Similarly, other studies examining personality development and adjustment (Winicott, 1952; Bowlby, 1980) highlight disruption in mother-infant relationships as being a prerequisite to vulnerability and adjustment difficulties in adult life.

Relationship difficulties

Birth parents talked of frequent relationship difficulties, particularly with new partners. Unresolved relationship problems with the other biological parent of their children appeared to inhibit intimacy. They often spoke of being isolated within new relationships due to the loss of children shared with the biological parent. It is interesting to note the findings of Bowlby's (1990) study of parents who lose children as a result of illness. He suggested that how well or how badly mourning proceeds is dependent on the parents' relationship and their ability to support one another in their grieving; where parents are in conflict and mutual support is absent, the death may lead to family break-up or psychiatric casualties.

Raphael (1983) comments on how others may enable grieving by sharing memories and events. Leslie, Alan and Mary had new partners who did not share losing the child, neither had they met the "lost" child. This may have prevented the new partners from being able to assist the bereavement process. Leslie feels anger towards her new partner. She said that she thought this was connected to feelings about her previous partner whom she blames for the loss of her first child. She talked of aggression towards her partner – hitting out at him. She was unable to give in the relationship. She referred to her present partner as a 'good man', 'good with Lisa' her second child but nevertheless there were difficulties related to the loss of her son.

My partner knows about my first child but I can't talk to him – I feel alone. He doesn't know my son, he's only heard about him. He says I can talk to him but I don't want to; he's my son and I lost him.

Alan expressed fears of getting into another relationship. He was concerned about needing to resolve problems in his past relationship with the mother of his children.

I need to sort myself out first.

He expressed ambivalence about intimacy:

She's a nice person — been there for me when I need someone I've helped her too but I don't love her. I have to sort my head out . . . I'm so confused.

Mary frequently talked of feeling trapped in a new relationship. She carried a lot of anger towards her previous partner, the father of her children, and still had many questions about how the relationship caused the removal of the children. She is unwilling to talk about it with her new partner as 'they're not his kids'. She accepts that she cannot get close to him as most of her is 'still with me kids'.

Studies examining how people cope with traumatic experiences highlight anger and irritability as features of psychological stress which may be directed at a partner who did not share the traumatic event. A feeling that comfort can only be gained from those with similar experiences may result in a partner feeling excluded or resentful (Hodgkinson and Stewart, 1991).

In addition, loss of a child through adoption and loss of parental status brings with them a sense of dislocation. Birth parents are faced with life which is different from the one they knew before. Raphael (p. 103) considered dislocation and relocation as arising from personal disasters, which result in loss of ideals as well as loved ones. She commented that a sense of dislocation can further complicate unresolved distress about events.

It may be that relationship difficulties faced by Leslie, Alan and Mary were precipitated by a profound sense of dislocation. This may be a way of explaining why Leslie could not transfer her loss of her adopted child into her new relationship, thus causing conflicts between her and her new partner.

Cath described problems which stemmed from establishing post-adoption contact with her children. Her new partner attempted to form a relationship with these children who rejected his attempts. They preferred to search for their birth father. Conflicts arose between the couple; as a result the birth mother queried the continuation of contact with her "adopted children".

A common area of stress for those who were in new relationships was fear of pregnancy or their partner wanting children which they did not. Sometimes birth parents were struggling to contain their anger at their partner's belief that a joint child would help them to make a new start and "get over it".

Difficulties in relationships extended to the parents' wider social group. Most post-adoptive birth parents felt that they had exhausted, or never had, the support of family and friends. They were expected to "forget" and "get on with life" which increased their fear that they were crazy to still feel the way they did.

Many birth parents said that their difficulties were related to their own mood swings. One mother described how suddenly, in the middle of a family gathering, she felt so isolated that she became violently angry and threw everyone out of the house. She knew that this was related to her deep misery about her children but for the family it was a sudden unprovoked outburst which later caused her problems with her partner. These conflicts tended to lead to the commonly expressed sentiment that 'it's safer to be on my own'.

This has important implications for social workers assessing family functioning with regard to subsequent children.

Parenting of subsequent children

Their capacity for bonding and attachment was a central issue for birth parents. They revealed their uncertainty by a fear of pregnancy or exaggerated concerns about the gender of subsequent children.

The effect of unresolved grief profoundly affected attachment and bonding. This was often anticipatory: Pam described how, while she was pregnant, she would frequently talk to her unborn child. The talking was purposeful; she repeatedly told the child who "he" was and all sorts of detailed information about the family. She felt that she had to ensure that "he" knew who he really was, lest

he was taken away. She also described how she had fought the mid-
wives on the delivery table because she felt her baby was only safe
with her while unborn.

Leslie requested sterilisation when she lost her legal battle for her
child. Fear of the removal of subsequent children understandably
dominated her thoughts and precipitated panic about pregnancy. This
inevitably had an impact on future relationships.

Jenny talked of the strain of relating to her second child, Kylie,
when she asked about her lost sibling. It had made her angry with
her daughter as it had set off painful memories which led to the
potential removal of Kylie. Her parenting abilities were immobilised,
leaving her frustrated, guilty and angry.

Jenny's anger and bitterness about the lack of an affectionate bond
with Kylie was evident. It is not clear how much this mother blamed
her for the loss of her first, but she did say that she was an unplanned
and unwanted child. She said that she 'can't bear to be there when
Kylie talks about Jason'. She also found it hard even to contemplate
holding a child of the same sex as the one removed. Bowlby in his
study of parents who lose children through illness found that blaming
a surviving child for the death of a sibling was particularly likely if
the death was sudden. It is interesting to note parallels in the circumstances of Jenny and those described by Bowlby. Jenny's first child,
Jason, was removed via a Place of Safety Order and did not return to
her care whilst Kylie remained. Openness from her nuclear and
extended family about her adopted child seemed to be important in
easing the situation for Jenny.

Alan's feelings of panic were triggered by the birth of a subsequent
child. His anxiety appeared to have two strands – the fear of becoming attached to this child in case of future loss, and guilt at bonding
with this child in the absence of the adopted children. He wished to
be present at the birth but it made him feel disloyal towards his
adopted children. He was not able to look at or hold the new born
child for several days.

I couldn't hold my son – I was so scared, scared of getting attached to him. I felt guilty – what would my other children think – would they feel pushed out? I need to tell them about this myself – I don't want social workers telling them things – I want them to hear it from me so I can explain they are still important to me.

Later he described overcoming these feelings once he could hold the baby. He is taking a primary role in this infant's care and bonding is observable. In counselling sessions Alan recognised that this child was not a replacement for children lost through adoption and acknowledged the fears provoked by the birth. It is interesting to note that Alan had a great need to be an involved father which appeared to be related to proving his parenting abilities.

Active parenting of a new-born baby may be Alan's attempt to correct the biases of his previous record as a parent. As Goffman (1963) stated, 'What often results is not the acquisition of a fully normal status (successful parenting), but a transformation of the self from someone with a particular blemish into someone with a record of having corrected the blemish'. (p 20).

Rose found it difficult initially to share any aspect of parenting her second child, Leanne. She had an anxious determination to bond that became fraught with the distress caused by the baby reminding her of the removed child. While she was grappling with all this, her parenting was being assessed by Social Services.

Cath did not report difficulties about parenting subsequent children, though she did mention that she was pleased that these children were a different gender to the ones she lost. She had always brought her daughters up in the knowledge of her "adopted sons". All the children now had contact with each other.

One mother was very conscious of the intensity of her feelings for her subsequent child, Paul. She talked of him being the only reason for her to live and that she would kill herself if anything happened to him. This same mother also talked of being treated as a new mum at the hospital or health centre despite the fact that she had parented four other children.

There were many concerns about how to explain the absence of adopted siblings to other children. There was no information available or knowledge offered about how best to approach this . Parents looked for help from the project. They sought assistance via counselling. Sue commented:

Hassan needs to see a picture of James so that Hassan can understand that James, the adopted child, didn't just simply disappear.

3 • The value of offering an independent counselling service

The findings of the pilot study in 1992 indicated a need for a counselling service for contesting birth parents. Initially we anticipated this would be primarily a post-adoption service, to help birth parents acknowledge their grief and the psychological impact of adoption on their lives. As the demand for the service grew, so did the demand for counselling throughout the process of adoption.

Those who requested counselling spoke of a 'desperate need for help'; 55 per cent of parents asked for counselling at the referral stage. The evaluation of the project showed that parents responded to the independent, non-judgmental, empathic approach offered (Mason and Selman, 1996), and our counselling records show that the counselling relationship lasted for an average of 10.5 months. Some parents received counselling for shorter periods and others for a maximum of two years. The frequency of sessions was negotiated at the contract stage to meet the needs of the individual. Sessions took place at a venue chosen by birth parents, principally in their own homes or in a neutral setting. We did not use venues that were in any way linked to social services departments.

Motivation for seeking counselling

Parents who were counselled for shorter periods, up to five sessions, had a strong desire to be heard. Those seeking counselling over a longer period could not cope with the effect on their lives of losing a child through compulsory adoption. Not being able to deal with their loss was made worse by resentment of injustice.

The main issues addressed in long-term counselling were:
1. The impact of loss and grieving: loss of a parent in childhood; abandonment and rejection by mother; abuse, violence, personal experience of being a child in care or adopted.

2. Parenting subsequent children.
3. Reaction to the adversarial nature of adoption.
4. Relationship difficulties.
5. Post-adoption contact.
6. Past life events and present life events: new partnerships, pregnancy, miscarriage, birth of another child. Current social services intervention.

Building on existing research

In the absence of studies relating specifically to the impact of compulsory adoption on birth parents, we reviewed research and the well documented experiences of relinquishing birth mothers to develop a framework for our understanding. In the past, two assumptions were made about mothers who relinquished their babies for adoption: firstly, that they did so in the child's and their own interests and secondly, that they would make an appropriate adjustment by putting it all behind them and getting on with their lives. With hindsight we know the decision to relinquish was closely related to societal attitudes toward illegitimacy, single parenting and financial considerations. Studies (Winkler and Van Heppel, 1984; Bouchier, Lambert and Triseloitis, 1991; Wells, 1990, 1993, 1994; Hughes and Logan, 1993) found evidence to suggest that relinquishing birth mothers, to varying degrees, experienced a form of grief which was life long and magnified by significant anniversaries and life events.

Group work with relinquishing birth mothers undertaken by the Post-adoption Centre in London (1990) confirmed these research findings and presented a more comprehensive picture than studies conducted by empirical methods. The Post Adoption Centre documented the birth mothers' shame, anger towards the system, the effects on parenting subsequent children, pain at not having more children, and dilemmas about not being able to tell people about their child after relinquishment. Further analysis of group themes provided information about the anguish suffered and the pathological effects such as post-natal and clinical depression as well as the difficulty in retaining an image of the child over time (p 4). Work with the group touched on social policy matters such as differences between society's views of adoptive parents and birth parents and issues of race, ethnicity, culture and class in relation to adoption placements.

The aforementioned studies and the work at the Post-adoption Centre indicate that adoption for most relinquishing birth mothers is perceived as a traumatic event. Research findings provide evidence that loss through adoption is affected by historical, cultural and social factors. Therefore to offer therapeutic services, including counselling, we need to have an understanding not only of loss and trauma but of the historical, cultural and social context in which this loss occurred.

The perspective of those experiencing compulsory adoption is further complicated by the legal process which enforces change and by its very nature creates stigma.

Loss

An extensive range of characteristics is associated with normal reactions to loss, mourning and active grief. However, mourning becomes pathological when adjustment to loss is not achieved. What would normally result in progressive healing leads to 'stereotyped repetitions or extensive interruptions of healing' (Horowitz *et al*, 1980). Pathological mourning has been associated with the life-long grief of relinquishing birth mothers (Millen and Roll, 1985).

Loss through adoption occurs over a prolonged period and therefore loss reactions can be observed in parents long before legal adoption takes place. For this reason we found it helpful to consider Bowlby's (1980) study of parental reactions to loss when children are diagnosed as terminally ill. Bowlby found that parents begin a process of mourning when the initial diagnosis is made. He observed a phase of numbness punctuated by bouts of anger while the child was still alive. Parents often disbelieved the diagnosis and prognosis. They frantically searched for information about the illness and attempted to prove the doctors wrong. They directed their anger at those responsible for making the diagnosis.

Similar stages can be observed in parents who learn of plans for their children to be adopted. Initially many parents disbelieve the decisions of case conferences, but at the same time they are frantically searching for legal information to know their rights, and to understand the train of events. Anger is mostly directed towards the workers who are planning the adoption. Following the phase of numbness, Bowlby found that parents went through a stage of anticipatory mourning during which they gradually detached themselves from their child. This was noted particularly when the illness was prolonged beyond four months, and led to a more resigned response to the child's death.

Similarly, a phase of anticipatory mourning can be observed in parents who are not able to keep up contact with their children when termination of contact is the eventual aim. These parents are likely to become detached from their children because they believe that the fight for their child is already over. Adoption with no form of contact may be experienced as a "living death" by the bereaved parents; a permanent loss without a real death.

Understanding individual differences in adjustment is important. Seligman (1995) related depression to helplessness. Orbach (1995) notes that the absence of external support can have a detrimental psychological effect if the person remembers events and situations that are 'denied or negated by others'. Parents may react to the loss of children in different ways. Studying parents who lost children through death, Hofter (*et al*, 1972) observed polarisation of responses. At one extreme were those who freely communicated their feelings about their loss and kept reminders of the child around them; at the other extreme there were some who appeared to show no signs of grieving and remained in control of their feelings. He found that physical symptoms were often presented by parents who were less likely to refer to their loss. These included headaches, palpitations, aches and pains, insomnia and unpleasant dreams.

Transitions following bereavement also involve dealing with secondary loss such as change in social role and identity. Parkes (1972) suggests this necessitates a review of one's self-image and the expectations of others.

Horowitz *et al* referred to four depressive states (fear, rage, shame and hibernation) as a normal grief reaction. They associated pathological grief with the inability to engage or complete the review of self-image, which Parkes believed is essential for coping with the changes in identity and social expectations. Horowitz concluded that for those affected individuals mourning is never completed.

Trauma

Post-traumatic stress disorder (PTSD) is mostly thought of as a reaction to natural or deliberate disasters. However, trauma is identified by many (Allinson 1991; Figley, 1988; Weiss and Payson, 1967) as the individual's psychological response to a catastrophic experience, which is so traumatic that it affects the individual's view of his or her world. What determines trauma for an individual depends on whether it is experienced as such. Birth parents appear to experience adoption as a traumatic event which threatens their psychological core.

Increasingly PTSD is recognised as a component of grief (Allinson, 1991; Parkes and Weiss, 1983; Parkes, 1972). Reliving the events of the trauma in thoughts or images are characteristic of PTSD. Flashbacks, distressing thoughts, images, illusions and hallucinations are symptoms of PTSD. The need to recount the events which led to removal of children and adoption was evident in almost all of our work with birth parents.

Sufferers of PTSD cannot resolve grief and are unwilling to address the effects of trauma which results in mood swings or depressive episodes that can become chronic. They will often seek to avoid places, feelings, thoughts and situations which trigger recall. Sadly one birth mother, whom we counselled about parenting a subsequent child, felt compelled to avoid the nursery in which she had last seen her adopted child. This meant she could not make use of the place offered for her second child. Social workers interpreted this as her not complying with the care plan for her younger child and had growing concerns about her ability to ensure that her child's needs were being met. When she had her next baby she began having terrible nightmares and anxiety attacks as her own birthday approached, marking the anniversary of her first child's removal. She described in counselling that she felt unable to disentangle the fear that her baby would be removed on that same day from the reassurance of the child care decision to let her keep her baby. The timing of the decision in this instance itself became a reminder of trauma. Wells (1993) attributed the inability of some birth mothers not to be able to recall events or the giving of consent to psychogenic amnesia: an extreme way of avoiding situations which awaken painful memories. Further attempts to dull emotions can result in dependency on drugs and alcohol. In extreme cases suicide becomes a means of escaping pain.

Some people feel detached or estranged, displaying guilt, lack of interest in usual activities or a vision of the future. Thompson (1989) described this as a 'psychic numbing'. Wells (1993) noted that secrecy surrounding adoptions perpetuates this state, a fact rarely acknowledged in child care cases.

The disruption caused by trauma can lead to isolation and alienation (Young and Erickson, 1989), though isolation may be seen as a way of coping by an attempt to avoid unwelcome reminders. However, the isolation of birth parents may also be related to stigma.

Recognition and treatment of PTSD is crucial to prevent long-term problems such as depression, alcoholism, attempted suicide, violence, psychosocial difficulties, and unemployment (Wells, 1993; Miller *et al*, 1992; Allinson, 1991; Kolb, 1989). Research indicates that peer support groups and counselling with psychiatric back up are the best forms of care; trust between the client and counsellor being an essential component of therapeutic help (Hillias and Cox in Allinson 1991).

Translating theory into practice

Despite our efforts we were not able to offer groupwork for birth parents, due to the wide geographical spread of our service users. We therefore provided counselling to individuals, couples and occasionally worked with family units. This enabled us to identify stages which relate to theory and the counselling tasks that other professionals can expect when engaging in similar work.

Our approach

Our person-centred approach to counselling placed emphasis on developing a therapeutic relationship which demonstrated respect, acceptance and empathy.

Respecting their autonomy, we believed birth parents could make appropriate choices about their need for counselling, the length of time they engaged in counselling, the frequency of sessions and the pace at which issues were addressed. Working in this way minimised conflicts and protected both workers and clients.

Stage I – Witnessing

Birth parents generally need to "tell their story" and to have this story witnessed by their counsellor. They often recount what has happened (usually the removal of the child) in minute detail. They may display irritability and anger at this stage, particularly when they have difficulty in recalling the exact time sequence of events. For many the action of the past seems to be set in the present. They will talk about physical reactions to trauma, recall retrieval dreams and talk about isolation from others. The counsellor therefore needs to acknowledge this as their present state, and may need to seek permission to liaise with psychiatric or medical services if these reactions are severe.

At this stage it is important that the counsellor actively witnesses the parent's story, feeding back to their client that they have heard and understood. This will help to make sense of events. In our experience the compulsion to go over and over the past may continue for a number of sessions and recur if the trauma is re-activated by anniversaries, birthdays or other such significant dates or events.

At the same time, birth parents must have their status validated. In many cases the need to tell their story was suspended in the second session by a more desperate need to have their identity confirmed. For this reason we encouraged birth parents to show family photographs of their children, thus acknowledging them as parents.

In the absence of a peer group we endeavoured to link parents with other parents at this stage, not only to provide support, but also to confirm that they were not alone in their distress.

Stage II – Impact

As parents begin to assimilate traumatic events, disbelief at what has happened often follows. This is consistent with the early stages of mourning and may coincide with talk about dreams that restore their parenting role. Parents may become distressed when this is not reality.

At this stage birth parents also describe feeling disconnected from their everyday lives, numb from their pain. This state can be punctuated by bouts of fury, usually directed towards the social worker allocated to their children. The anger is often voiced as: 'she wanted my children'.

The task of counselling at this stage is to maintain empathy and acceptance.

Stage III – Acknowledging loss of the child

Talk about the actual loss of their child brings with it a realisation of the birth parents' changed role and identity. At this stage parents will frequently be angry, talk of injustice and intensify their fight for their child (if the Adoption Order has not been made). They will often request information about adoption, look for advocates or review their legal representation. The counsellor is required to acknowledge their feeling and to provide information to enable birth parents to make informed choices about courses of action they could take.

It is very important that the counsellor recognises that this is another stage of mourning and is clear about his or her role, which is not to protect the adoptive placement from potential risk. Based on our experience, this is for two reasons. Firstly, we have not come across any birth parent who intended to retrieve the child from their adoptive placements, despite many parents knowing of their child's whereabouts, because they understand the detrimental effect it would have on their child. Secondly, searching behaviour is associated with pining and usually implies that they know their child is lost.

It is at this stage that parents appear more susceptible to depression, talk of suicidal thoughts (and in extreme cases makes attempts) or display high states of arousal. The task of the counsellor is to acknowledge the impact of their loss and to allow the anger to come out, even when it threatens to turn into action. How this is treated within the therapeutic relationship is crucial. Counsellors need to be aware of the limitations of confidentiality if their clients are at risk of harming themselves or others, and have a duty to inform the client of any proposed actions that would break confidentiality if this were deemed to be ethically appropriate. However, birth parents need to be able to express anger about their loss in a safe environment that demonstrates acceptance of all parts of them. For some parents it was helpful to admit that one part of them felt like acting out their rage, while another part knew this was not acceptable.

In our experience, working in depth with rage requires the counsellor to maintain congruence with the client at all times: to reflect changes in facial expressions, body language and eye contact.

It is helpful to alert the client to what is happening; increased awareness can lead to inner integration and build up a sense of self so that
eventually angry feelings can be controlled and not acted upon.

This can be illustrated by an extract from a session with a birth
father:

Counsellor	'I feel frightened (maintenance of congruence), you look different, your body looks tense and your face looks different.'
Stephen	(Looks at counsellor, had previously disengaged from eye contact.)
Counsellor	'What's happening – notice what your body feels like.'
Stephen	'I feel tense.' (clenched fists – no eye contact)
Counsellor	'And what else?'
Stephen	'I feel like I'm going to explode, I'm shaking.'
Counsellor	'You're tense and you're shaking, you feel like you're going to explode (reflecting back), but these are seri-ous threats and I'm worried . . . it's like I don't know this side of you' (congruence).
Stephen	'When I lose it I don't know who I am.'
Counsellor	'So when you are really angry you lose a sense of other bits of yourself . . . I guess (tentatively) that's frightening.'
Stephen	'I'm scared, I'm scared of myself.' (begins to shake)
Counsellor	'It's scary when you lose touch, it's scary for me too (maintaining congruence). I wonder if we can have the other bit of you here too (counsellor pulls up a chair close to him) as there is another bit of you that wants to get hold of this. Can you acknowledge that bit too?'

This extract demonstrates how the counsellor, by maintaining congruence with the client, draws on ways of being able to ground
Stephen and have him become aware of other bits of himself. At no

time is the counsellor passing judgement on the client. The session continues with Stephen looking directly at the empty chair as if at another side of himself, and he moves on to describe the other, calmer, part of himself. Working like this obviously requires the counsellor to have a good understanding of therapeutic processes, and to feel confident about the safety of the client and her or himself. Counsellors have a responsibility to work at a level to match their experience. A very skilled counsellor worked with this particular birth father, but the record may provide useful pointers for others offering support services to birth parents.

Working with suicidal thoughts and actions
Counsellors need to be aware that many birth parents deal with their pain by suicidal thoughts or actions. In our experience this is a reaction to court and early legal proceedings.

Birth parents not only have to accept a change of role, they must also live with a change in public status; they are no longer being seen as parents. These secondary losses produce low self-esteem. It is not unusual at this stage for parents to bring to counselling dilemmas about how to handle public enquiries such as 'have you got any children?' or 'how are your kids?'. This could be an indication that parents who were previously socially isolated are now seeking social interactions.

Of course there are no easy solutions and the task in counselling is to help parents explore different options open to them for coping in public. Loss through adoption is devoid of ritual to mark loss or remembrance. Therefore, part of the therapeutic work may be to help birth parents develop a ritual whereby the child can be remembered and his or her life celebrated. Some parents find their own rituals naturally, others need "permission" and encouragement. For example, we explained to one mother the slogan behind the Natural Parents Support Group – elephants never forget – and provided her with an elephant-shaped candle to light in remembrance of her daughter at Christmas.

Post-adoption contact has therapeutic value but birth parents have to feel worthy in order to contribute to their children's lives. They should be supported in their post-adoption contact and be given the opportunity to provide information for their children, as far as possible uncontaminated by the hostility that often exists in compulsory situations.

Counsellors can support birth parents in their initial post-adoption contact. Fears and fantasies about the adoptive parents are dispelled by face-to-face meetings, but where this is not possible, counsellors can help birth parents to address their fears and fantasies through role play with the birth parent becoming both the adoptive parents and their own child. Sharing the post- adoption information brought by parents to session can be equally therapeutic and enhancing to their self-worth.

Suicide has been strongly linked to family breakdown (Durkheim, 1897 trans: 1952), and may equally be attributable to changes in family structures as a result of statutory intervention: loss of child/ren, consequently loss of partners and loss of parental status. Suicidal actions may also result from self-reproach if anger leads to self-harm.

When suicidal thoughts are expressed, counsellors must assess the risk to ensure client safety and, if appropriate, enable them to receive support from other parents or professionals. It is important to work with psychiatric backing if necessary.

Depression is often a feature during this stage and follows periods of intense pining for the child. It may also follow court proceedings, or termination of face-to-face contact because these events emphasise the parents' helplessness to affect their situation. Birth parents who have become isolated or who have their experiences denied by others are particularly vulnerable. The aim of counselling is to validate their experience and to acknowledge their grief. Linking with other contesting parents can strengthen the counselling service.

Stage IV – Living with the loss

Focusing on the birth parents' perspective should make counsellors be aware that birth parents rarely accept the loss of their child through adoption, therefore the process of coming to terms with their loss is more about finding ways of living with it than about moving towards acceptance.

Counsellors supporting and understanding mourning parents need to know about the psychosocial effects of change as well as the complexities of grief.

Living with their loss means that birth parents have to accommodate a change of role in relation to their child. Adoption separates the parenting and legal responsibilities from the genetic and blood tie relationship (Fahlberg, 1981); that is why birth parents should have a continuing role in helping children to maintain a complete sense of identity.

Counselling support

The role of counselling at this stage may be to support birth parents to explore a different relationship with their child in future years as well as assisting birth parents to develop an identity for themselves which enables them to understand and live with loss through adoption.

It is important that workers are not disabled by the pain of witnessing trauma. It can be harrowing and exhausting to work in depth with the grief of birth parents. The loss of children is a highly emotive subject and can trigger remembrance of loss in all of us. There is also a danger that the counsellor may try to rescue the parent and take up their fight instead of empowering the parent through counselling. As it is evident that birth parents need both counselling and advocacy, preserving a boundary between the two is crucial.

For this reason we found it helpful to set up counselling supervision, in accordance with the British Association of Counselling

(BAC) guidelines, with an experienced and accredited supervisor. Supervision also gave us additional support when we were working with clients who were expressing rage and offered us a forum to discuss ways of managing difficult situations as well as ethical dilemmas about client safety or the safety of others arising out of the counselling relationship. Counselling supervision was set up outside the normal line management structures.

4 • The value of offering other independent services

In addition to counselling the project offered a number of other services.

Providing information

Parents contacted the project for information about adoption. Whilst information about adoption and the legal stages may have been provided by local authority social workers or solicitors, birth parents, either through lack of trust or their emotional state at the time, may not have been able to take in the information given to them. They reported difficulty in understanding the terminology used by their solicitors. They felt confused about the purpose of child care planning meetings and were unclear about the part played by professionals.

Many birth parents asked for specific information relating to their particular circumstances. In these instances oral explanations were later followed by a written explanation appropriate to the birth parents' understanding.

Fact sheets were another useful way of providing general information about adoption and parents' rights. We also encouraged birth parents to seek information from other sources like the Family Rights Groups and legal advocacy projects, by providing them with a list of helpful organisations and contact registers. Parents seeking advice about legal representation were supplied with the names of solicitors currently on the child care panel within their area.

As our referrals increased we became clearer about the type of information birth parents need if they are to participate in planning for their children. This can be summarised as:

1. Explanation of
   - Case conferences.
   - Parental attendance at conferences.
   - Legal Orders – Care Order
     Freeing Order
     Adoption Order
     Contact Order
     Section 8 Order
   - Dispensing with consent.
   - Rights of appeal.
   - How the local authority plans for permanence – the various legal routes to securing a child's safety.
   - Issues of openness in adoption – details of why information exchange, direct or indirect contact may be part of the plan for their child.
   - How adoptive parents are chosen, assessed and prepared.
   - Legal rights of the child to know of their origin.
   - Adoption records.
   - Preparing and supporting of their child – lifestory work.

2. Information about departmental policies on:
   - Meeting adoptive parents.
   - Post-adoption contact.
   - Letterbox contact.
   - Post-adoption service to birth parents.

3. Knowledge of legal and social work practice regarding contact:
   - Birth parents are not always aware that contact and information exchange are dependent on the views and wishes of the adoptive family post-adoption and that any pre-adoption agreement is difficult to enforce.
   - Parents need to know how the department works to prepare and support the child if contact is terminated.

4. Information about the role of the Guardian *ad Litem*:
   - How they are appointed.
   - What their task entails.

5. Information about giving or not giving consent:
   - Parents' rights.
   - How consent is sought and by whom.
   - What happens if parents do not give consent.

6. Contact registers:
   - Printed information leaflets.
   - How help can be found if needed.
   - Costs involved.

Much of the information we provided about adoption practice could be made available by statutory agencies. However, there is a role for independent advocates to support parents during the adoption process. In the course of our work we found that some local authorities did offer such a service via adoption social workers. This was well received by birth parents who appreciated a visit from a specialist in adoption, particularly as many parents felt adoption social workers were more receptive to the idea of post-adoption contact than the child's worker who was caught up in planning for permanence.

Using role play in preparation for case conferences

Within a therapeutic relationship the use of role play for conferences was explored. Parents found this technique helpful, not only to prepare what they wanted to say, but also to take the part of the social worker, health visitor or teacher. By playing different roles in the case conference parents were able to gain an understanding of different views held about their children's welfare. In some instances they could confront difficulties they had in protecting their children or promoting their welfare and propose strategies for dealing with concerns.

Preparation for role play included information about how the case conference would be managed (the counsellor finding this out in advance), clarification about the use of an advocate/friend/supporter and working out what the birth parent wanted to present to the conference. This enabled some parents to be active participants in case conferences, to represent themselves more adequately or to find suitable advocates. In one case, birth parents noted the concerns of the local authority about their children witnessing marital violence, and realised that this was something they could work on and thereby prevent the registration of their other children.

This area of work could have been further developed, if we had more resources, to include preparation for court and meetings with adoptive parents.

Video work with birth parents

One of the services we provided for birth parents was the chance to make a video for their children. This was offered to all birth parents. The video could either be placed on the child's adoption file, or ideally, be forwarded to their children via their adoptive parents and social services.

Many birth parents took this opportunity as a way of talking directly to their children. To get over the nervousness of appearing before a camera parents were given time to practice informally or to use the camera themselves. This was particularly successful when other family members were involved. Grown up siblings often took on the job of filming, introducing their parents to their adopted brothers and sisters. This medium enabled parents to show family photograph albums with a running commentary about life events, family relationships and subsequent family developments. It provided a wealth of information for their adopted children which could not easily be recorded in lifestory books. Birth parents found the process therapeutic and empowering as they could talk to their children of their feelings about the adoption and their perception of the events leading up to it. Making a video gave siblings who had remained within their family a chance to face their loss and feelings about relationships that had been disrupted by adoption.

We found there was an immediacy about the way birth parents spoke on camera, as if they were really speaking directly to their children. They talked frankly about the mistakes they felt they had made and, in some cases, expressed disbelief at the sequence of events that had led to their children being removed from their care. With hindsight parents were often able to tell their children 'what should have been different', and thereby to work through years of guilt.

Parents whose children were in closed adoptions could speak of their grief and tell their children about the impact adoption had on their lives, the guilt they felt at being able to care for subsequent children, or the dilemmas they faced when publicly appearing child-less and yet longing to acknowledge their adopted children. Video work gave Joanne, like some other parents, the opportunity to talk to her children about her inability to protect them due to personal fears and immaturity. She also talked freely about how she felt when her children were sexually abused by her then boyfriend. She explained why she originally alerted the authorities to her suspicions.

This particular work led us to appreciate how much parents are willing and able to be a resource to their adopted children and to what extent they become inhibited by their relationship with statutory agencies. The preparation of videos had obvious therapeutic benefits for birth parents. They could hear themselves, review their own perceptions, and believe that they still had a role to play in their children's lives. This ultimately raised their self-esteem.

Helping birth parents to be a resource to their children placed for adoption

Lifestory work

We received many third party requests to help parents to prepare lifestory books for their children, but also in the course of counselling, the parents' desire to provide information for their children was a regular issue. Many birth parents were angry about being asked for photographs of their children by social workers who were associated with their removal, and referred to it as a final stripping of everything they had left 'they even want your memories . . . and that's all I have left'. This was clearly more an indication of how they felt about the adversarial relationship than of any unwillingness to be a resource to their children. They did not want a social worker to decide how things should be told to their child. Separated from their hostile feelings about social services, parents were mindful of their children's needs and generously gave information about their children's early lives, as well as photographs, and in some cases found mementoes for their child such as birthday cards. These things were given freely, though not without comment that they would not have been given directly to social workers.

Some birth parents wished to include photographs taken during pregnancy scans (best reproduced by a colour photocopy). These photocopies meant recognition of their part in their child's identity, as Lisa commented:

> *He'll be able to see he grew inside of me, I think that will help him understand who he is. He's a part of me even if he's living with someone else . . . maybe they* (adoptive parents) *might be able to explain his adoption better too.*

Completing lifestory work with birth parents was not without problems for us. The timing of this work is crucial, as it is easily affected by the birth parents' feelings about the legal process of adoption. In some cases it was difficult to have consent for the books to be given to social services if it coincided with legal stages, such as 'freeing', which confirmed the loss of the child and the finality of adoption. Requests for a book to be passed on at this stage seemed to invoke a feeling of 'winner takes all'. We learned to discuss consent at a much earlier stage and to warn birth parents that their feelings could obstruct the purpose of making such a book. Knowing how difficult it was for some parents to complete these life stories, even when they wanted to, we felt it was important to photograph the process of making them, as well as copying the completed book, for parents to have a record of what they had done.

Once passed on to social services, we requested a formal receipt for the lifestory books which in turn were given directly to birth parents and not kept for our records. In short, we perceived our role to be merely as intermediaries.

Letter to the child to be read at a later stage
Whilst most parents had been asked to write a letter for their child by social workers handling the adoption, many felt constrained about what they could say in these letters. They felt they could not write about their reasons for not consenting to the adoption in case this prevented a letter being passed to their child in the future. Yet the need to explain about consent came up frequently during lifestory work; not only for the benefit of their children but also for the adoptive parents.

For those who had not written a letter at the time of their child's adoption, the possibility of placing something on the adoption file, at a later stage, offered the opportunity to "finish business" that had disturbed them for some time. Evelyn freely admitted that she had been unable to write anything at the time of her third child's adoption but asked for help to do so now as she had heard adoptions were more open. Her letter simply stated:

I met your adoptive mam and dad. They cried. So did I because we all love you.

With some letters as in the case of Evelyn, our role was principally one of facilitator: to recognise that parents needed permission to go ahead with something that troubled them, and then to mediate with social services about placing it on file. In the main, local authorities were positive about placing information on adoption files and in a few cases, to our knowledge, alerted adoptive parents that this information had been received.

Conclusion

The services we offered were in recognition of an unmet need. Over a three year period we were able to demonstrate demand and develop a range of services that met birth parents' needs for support as well as advocacy.

Birth parents responded to the independent nature of the project as well as its person-centred approach. The approach encouraged birth parents both to seek help and to participate in the development of services. This is evident from the many letters we received:

I have had counselling from Parents without Children for a total of two years. I was put in touch with them through a flyer on the wall at social services. At first I thought this organisation would stand up for me and help me that way, but I found I was wrong. What I did get out of it was the counselling help to clear my mind, because I was confused and I didn't know which way to turn. When something as traumatic as this happens to you it messes up your mind and makes you feel isolated and vulnerable.

Barry

. . . personally I thought Parents without Children was an enormous help. The counselling I received was both a pleasure and informative, with dramatic results. I have learned how to cope with my problems, how to face

them head on. Before I started counselling I was all mixed up. I didn't know where my priorities lay. I didn't know how to face my problems and I used to hide from them. Now I can sit down and sort them out. I know that I have to because problems like I had would never have gone away.

When I turned up to see my counsellor I looked forward to it because if I was not sure about something, I'd ask. I'm quite happy with the way she explained things to me.

I am now a confident young lady, I'm learning through my counselling how to enjoy life because before I didn't have any confidence or knowledge on how to tackle the past. I felt like everything in my life was my fault. I've had bad experiences in relationships, I never knew why but now I know. . . I realised these patterns through my counselling. I have never, never been able to talk freely to anyone before. I was a bit dubious about counselling. I've never been totally honest with anybody before and at first I was a bit scared. It's totally confidential which I think is super.

I'm on the mend now but I know I will need counselling for a long time yet . . .

Mandy

Parents without Children grew out of the work of an established adoption agency, but as it developed it became increasingly more difficult for this kind of project to be a part of an agency whose main focus of work is dominated by an emphasis on the other parties in the celebration of adoption. Conflicts which arose led us to believe that services for birth parents, who lose their children against their wishes, would be better placed either as a completely independent organisation or within an agency whose work deals with the impact of adoption on the lives of all the parties involved.

Sadly, despite continued support from Henry Smith's Charity, we were unable to secure sufficient funds to continue our work, but we hope our experience, along with the findings of the researchers who worked with us (Mason and Selman, 1996), will enable other agencies to meet this need.

References

Adcock M, Kanuick J and White R, *Exploring Openness in Adoption*, BAAF, pp 7–24, 37–78, 1993.

Allinson A J, 'Post-traumatic Stress Disorder: A British Perspective' in *Med. Sci. Law*, 31:3, 1991.

Bartrop R W, Lazarus L, Luckhurst E, Kiloch L G and Penny R, 'Depressed Lymphocyte Function after Bereavement', *Lancet*, 16.4, 8.34–36, 1977.

Bouchier P, Lambert L and Triseliotis J, '*Parting with a Child for Adoption*', pp 55–95, BAAF, 1991.

Bowlby J, *Attachment and Loss: Vol 3, Loss, sadness and depression*, Penguin Educational, Ch 7, 1981.

Bowlby J, *The Making and Breaking of Affectional Bonds*, Tavistock, 1984.

Burnell A, 'Exploring Open Adoption: a post adoption perspective', pp 79–89, in *Exploring Openness in Adoption*, Significant Publications, 1993.

Department of Health, *Review of Adoption Law*, HMSO, 1992.

Driver G and Miles J, 'Babylon Laws', in O'Shaughnessy T, *Adoption, Social Work and Social Theory*, Avebury, 1994.

Durkhiem E, *Suicide: A study in sociology*, Trans: Spaulding and Simpson, Routledge in Parkes C M, *Bereavement: Studies of grief in adult life*, 1972, Pelican, 1952.

Figley C R, in McCann I L and Pearlman L A, *Psychological Trauma and the Adult Survivor*, Bruner/Mazel, 1988 and 1990, USA.

Goffman E, *Stigma*, Pelican, 1963.

Gorer G, *Death, Grief and Mourning in Contemporary Britain*, Tavistock, 1965.

Hodgkinson P E and Stewart M, *Coping with Catastrophe*, Routledge, 1991.

Hofer M A, Wolff C T, Friedman S B and Mason J W, 'A Psychoendocrine Study of Bereavement', *Psychosomat Med* 34, 481–504, 1972.

Hughes B and Logan J, *Birth Parents: The hidden dimension*, Department of Social Policy and Social Work, University of Manchester, 1993.

Lawson E, 'Contested adoption proceedings: A barrister's perspective', (p 46 and p 48) in Ryburn M, *Contested Adoptions*, Arena, 1994.

Linderman E, 'The symptomatology and Management of Acute Grief' in *American Journal of Psychiatry*, 101:141, 1944.

Mardi J, Horowitz M D, Wilner W, Marmar C and Krupwick M S W, 'Pathological Grief and the Activation of Latent self-image', in *American Journal of Psychiatry*, 137, 10 October 1980.

Mason K and Selman P, *Parents Without Children: An evaluation and research report*, Department of Social Policy, Newcastle University, 1996.

McCann I L and Pearlman L A, *Psychological Trauma and the Adult Survivor*, Bruner/Mazel, 1990, USA.

Millen L and Roll S, 'Solomon's Mothers: A special case of pathological bereavement', in *American Journal of Orthopsychiatry*, 55, 411–418, 1985, USA.

Miller T W, Kamenchenko P and Karasniashski A, 'Assessment of Life Stress Events: The aetiology and measurement of traumatic stress disorder' in *The International Journal of Social Psychiatry*, 38:3, pp 215–227, 1992.

Mullender A (ed), *Open Adoption: The philosophy and practice*, BAAF, 1991.

Orbach S, 'When it's all about self, self, self' in the *Guardian Weekend* 13.5.95.

Parkes C M, *Bereavement: Studies of grief in adult life*, Pelican, 1972.

Parkes C M and Weiss R, *Recovery from Bereavement*, Basic Books, 1983.

Raphael B, *When Disaster Strikes*, Unwin Hyman, 1983.

Rendal S, *Birth Parents and Adoption: A study of social work services for parents who give up a child for adoption*, MA Thesis, Sunderland University, 1993.

Ryburn M, *Contested Adoptions: Research, law, policy and practice*, Arena, 1994.

Ryburn M, 'Contact after contested adoptions', *in Adoption & Fostering*, 18:4, 1994.

Seligman M E P, *Helplessness*, Freeman, 1975, USA.

Smart and Young in Ryburn M, *Contested Adoptions: Research, law, policy and practice*, Arena, 1994.

Spinelli E, *The Interpreted World: An introduction to phenomenological psychology*, Sage, 1989.

Thompson C, in Allinson A J, 'Post-traumatic stress disorder: A British Perspective', *Med. Sci. Law*, 31:3, 1991.

Tye L, *Birth parents talk back*, Cramlington: Birth parents/adoptees support group, 1994.

Warden J W, *Grief Counselling and Grief Therapy*, Tavistock, 1982.

Weiss R J and Payson H E, in McCann I L and Pearlman L A, *Psychological Trauma and the Adult Survivor*, Brunner/Hazel, 1990, USA.

Wells S, 'On becoming a birth mother', in *Adoption & Fostering*, 14:2, pp 45–47, 1990.

Wells S, 'What do birth mothers want?' in *Adoption & Fostering*, 17:4, 1993.

Wells S, 'Post-traumatic stress disorder in birth mothers' in *Adoption & Fostering*, 17:2, 1993.

Wells S, 'The agony and the ecstasy' in *The Guardian*, 6.9.93.

Wells S, *Within me, Without me: Adoption – an open and shut case?* Scarlet Press, 1994.

Winnicott C, '*Anxiety associated with insecurity*', in Winnicott Collected Papers, Tavistock, 1958, 1952.

Winkler R and van Keppel M, *Relinquishing Mothers in Adoption: Their long-term adjustment*, Melbourne: Institute for Family Studies, Monograph, No 3, 1984, Australia.

Young M B and Erickson C A, 'Cultural impediments: PTSD in contemporary America', in *Journal of Traumatic Stress* 1 (4) 431–443, 1989.

PART 2 • BEFORE ADOPTION

Maureen Crank and Kinni Kansara

5 • Introduction

This paper describes the work of the *Before Adoption* project which came about in response to a need identified during the work of *After Adoption* in Manchester. *After Adoption* is a small voluntary agency that opened its doors to the public in December 1990. It offers post-adoption services to all parties after adoption: birth parents, adopted people and adoptive parents. Initial services to birth parents (ie. parents who have lost a child to adoption) were funded by the Mental Health Foundation, which also commissioned independent research into the work with birth parents (Hughes and Logan, 1993).

This research was based on 100 birth parents who had used *After Adoption*'s services during a specified period of time. A very small percentage of these were parents who had lost their children to adoption through the care system. These people had very special needs which appeared not to be met by any agency. Often they were so angry, or had such low self-esteem, that they had great difficulty in accessing any help and they needed a service to address their particular situation. Having raised these issues, *After Adoption* approached several Trusts for grants to work with this group and in June 1994 the Nuffield Foundation provided money to fund the project for two years. In September 1994 the *Before Adoption* project worker was appointed.

Background

Many social workers attempt to offer support to birth parents who are opposed to the actions of social services, but this is extremely difficult and problematic because of the conflictual relationship and the way the child protection system separates off the child's best interests from the needs of parents. The social worker's role is primarily to identify children's needs, most often in the context of parental failings. The parents are mostly single mothers, living on the margins of society, often in extreme poverty. Nearly all the birth mothers and birth fathers who contacted the project lived in poor housing, on benefits, had a low level of basic education and limited access to employment, childcare and emotional and practical support.

An indication that birth parents' needs have been neglected within the current child protection system was confirmed in findings by the Social Services Inspectorate of adoption services in three local authorities in the North of England in 1992. Their report stated that there was evidence in the agencies inspected that there were considerable difficulties for social services offering counselling to contesting birth parents. It pointed to a clear need for authorities to consider alternative forms of counselling for birth parents who are in conflict with social services.

The process of losing their children through care proceedings left birth parents feeling completely powerless because social workers had intervened in their family and assessed them as being unfit to look after, and care for, their own children. Birth mothers have spoken with intensity of the loss they are left to carry on their own and the social stigma attached to being mothers who have lost their children through the care system to adoption. It often appears to the birth family that the purpose of this action is to point out and highlight a birth parent's perceived failings.

Establishing the project

The project was named *Before Adoption* to identify the work as being different from the "core" work of *After Adoption*: it would be mainly with birth parents *before* adoption, but *after* a decision for the children to be placed permanently with another family had been made.

Due to limited resources it was decided to confine the operation of the project to urban areas. This was to ensure that:

a) the project was not swamped with referrals;

b) workers did not spend their limited time travelling;

c) as all local authorities have different policies and procedures, it would not be too time consuming for any worker to get to know them.

The project would operate in local authority areas where *After Adoption* had a good working relationship. This would aid the local authority workers' understanding of the reasons for the project's involvement.

The first six months were spent in clarifying the value base of the project and in defining the aims and objectives as listed below.

The service aims

- To provide a person-centred counselling service to birth parents in which parents can explore issues around the loss of their children as well as other life events and losses such as childhood experiences, abuse, relationships and discrimination.
- To provide a service that is independent and confidential.
- To provide information and help to clarify the relevant legal and social work processes.
- To work with parents in negotiating a level of openness in the adoption arrangements for their child.
- To support parents in producing lifestory books, videos and tapes of themselves and their families for themselves and their children.
- To work with parents in exploring the role they can play in their children's lives both before and after adoption and support them in negotiations with social services in this respect.

- To raise awareness about the experiences of birth parents in contested proceedings and so inform legal and social work practice.

The above aims were redefined over the life of the project as the project worker began to learn from the experiences of the birth parents who came from different backgrounds and were at different stages in the social work and legal processes.

Developing aims and boundaries for the project and a method of working was difficult and challenging, since it meant reviewing the role of the worker in light of the requests made by birth parents concerning their needs and rights as well as being responsive to issues raised by the social services departments, which feared that the project would become advocacy work with birth parents.

A referral network was established which included:

- producing a publicity leaflet;
- distributing the leaflet around a wide variety of agencies which would be likely to have contact with birth parents, eg. mental health centres, clinics, GP surgeries;
- visits to voluntary agencies and social services to raise awareness of the project;
- visits to particular agencies whose users may struggle to get access to the project, eg. minority ethnic organisations and organisations dealing with people with disabilities.

Next came the definition of services to be provided:

- a counselling service;
- an information service; and
- an appropriate support service.

Clarifying boundaries for each of these services was a major task: the complexity of losing a child through adoption and other life losses associated with poverty and deprivation influence policy; for instance, does the support involve attending case conferences, planning meetings and so on?

Consultancy

A consultation group was set up of representatives from social services in the areas in which the project was to operate. The terms of reference for this group were established and later on in the project, the group was redefined as an *Information Exchange Group*.

Fundamental principles

It was felt important that the project make clear its value base for potential users of the service and for agencies, in order to encourage direct referrals and to support the development of practice that takes account of the position of contesting birth parents. The principles laid out were:

- All parents are parents for life even if they are unable to live with and care for their children on a day-to-day basis.
- Birth parents and children who are separated permanently have the right to maintain contact with each other. This can mean different levels of contact from regular exchange of information to direct face-to-face contact.
- Birth parents have the right to be well informed about legal and social work processes so that they can be clear about the long-term implications for them and their families.
- Birth parents should be offered, if they wish, practical and emotional support which is independent from social services, confidential and non-judgmental and which does not further stigmatise and undermine them as individuals and as parents.

These principles, incorporated in the project's publicity leaflet, are based on an understanding of the losses inherent in adoption, the view of birth parents, the complexity of contested proceedings and the impact of these proceedings on birth parents and children.

Referrals to the project

As already stated, the initial work including setting up a referral network which collated information on relevant organisations in order to send publicity material; contact with social services had already been established in Tameside, Salford, Stockport, Bolton and Manchester. Contact had also been made with some solicitors and guardians *ad litem*. Minority ethnic mental health projects were specifically targeted to ensure that minority groups could access the service. Before the task was complete, referrals started coming in and the project soon had an active caseload of parents who wanted to use the service. It was decided not to continue the publicity since it appeared the project could become inundated with referrals. It was not appropriate to raise expectations that a service could be provided when we were limited by only having one worker.

Referrals were accepted by the project on the basis that care plans had been made for children to be placed for adoption and birth parents were opposing them and wanted to contest them.

Breakdown of referrals

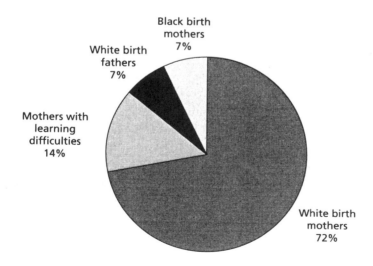

Length of counselling involvement

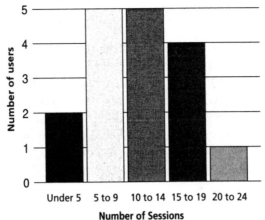

The information represented in the figures has been drawn from the in-depth work with birth mothers who have engaged in counselling. Most of the mothers had a combination of the above factors to deal with, apart from facing the trauma of contested adoption proceedings. They also had limited access to support from family, community or professional agencies. It is interesting to note that many of the stress factors in the lives of the birth mothers are used, by assessing social workers, to build the case as to why children should be removed from parents. It is clear that children need protection from abusive mothers or fathers. Children also need help with coming to terms with the loss of their parents and to understand that insufficient family, community and personal support is provided to parents to help them deal with the issues that have affected their parenting capacities.

Mira is a young woman who had four children removed from her by the age of 23 years, two of whom were removed soon after birth. She talked of her feelings to the project worker:

Social background and context

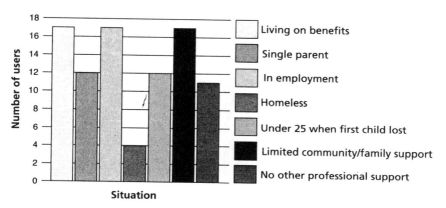

What is the point? . . . All I have ever wanted was my own family. . . I can't keep producing children for social services to take away from me. I can't keep going through the hurt and pain of it again and again. They take my children and then they just leave me to get on with life. When my last child was born, they took her straight from birth – even though I had planned for her and checked with social services before conception.

This young woman was considering sterilisation to ensure that she would not have to face the loss of yet another child against her will. She had been labelled as mentally ill. Her life experiences included a breakdown in her adoptive family, being in care and domestic violence as well as emotional and physical abuse in childhood. It is not surprising she had mental health problems. The question that comes to mind in each scenario with each birth mother is: what level of support was she offered to help her deal with the problems that led to the loss of her children? Problems that include a whole range of highly stressful circumstances apart from the removal of children, such as living in poverty, homelessness, dealing with the impact of

Personal situation within which children lost to adoption

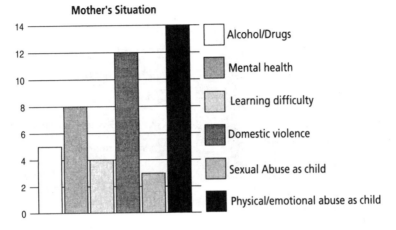

discrimination on the grounds of "race" and disability, limited or no support networks, or sexual, physical and emotional abuse in childhood and in subsequent relationships.

Counselling, information and support work

It was hoped that by working with birth parents who were in conflict with the local authority's plans for their children, the parents could be supported in terms of getting access to information, understanding and questioning the adoption process, having the space to talk through their feelings about what is happening and discussing the range of possibilities open to them. The aim was to enable parents to communicate with social services about the role they could play in their children's lives before and after they were permanently separated.

The themes of worthlessness, guilt, anger and hopelessness were touched upon during counselling sessions in varying degrees of depth. Mothers could explore the effect on themselves of both the

Children's Situation

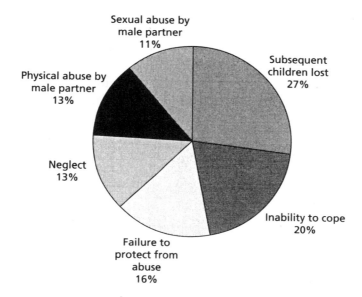

Sexual abuse by male partner 11%

Physical abuse by male partner 13%

Neglect 13%

Failure to protect from abuse 16%

Subsequent children lost 27%

Inability to cope 20%

loss of their children and their fight to prevent their children being adopted. At the initial stage of counselling many women wanted to check that information shared would not be reported back to social services. Mothers wanted confidentiality to be confirmed and the boundaries of confidentiality were agreed. As a result of women's life experiences and the extent and depth of their losses, counselling was very painful. Sometimes mothers would engage for a period of time and then have a break before being ready to allow some of their pain to resurface.

The counselling process was complicated by the differing needs for information and support which often came up at the same time because parents were at various stages of the legal and social work process.

The feelings of betrayal by social services and support agencies, the shock of their children being removed from their care, in a country where they were an ethnic and cultural minority, intensified their fears as to what would happen to their children and themselves. For one birth mother who did not speak English, feelings of isolation and alienation were further reinforced. Her own extended family networks were in India. Working through interpreters in an attempt to establish a sensitive communication process, did not reassure her. How could a woman in her position access non-judgmental, culturally appropriate individual and community support services?

Joanna

Joanna's daughter, Julie, had been taken into care after violence from an ex-partner approximately five years previously. Julie has special educational needs and was in foster care. She had been moved from one foster home to another and the most dependable figure in Julie's life was Joanna who had been visiting Julie weekly throughout the five years. Joanna was fiercely contesting adoption plans for Julie. Her circumstances had changed. She had left her violent ex-partner shortly after Julie had been taken into care. She had got married and was in a settled and supportive relationship. She had a second child, Thomas, who always visited Julie with his mother. Joanna wanted Julie returned home. Social services, however, planned for her to be long-term fostered or adopted and they had been seeking carers or adopters who would accept an open adoption. They did not think that Joanna, whom they considered to be short-tempered, would be able to cope with two children with special needs.

Joanna spoke bitterly of the court hearings and the whole process she had been through:

Social workers have been able to go back to my school records to build up a picture of me as a volatile and disruptive person who has been through many traumatic experiences. They have used this to say that because of childhood abuse, I will find it too difficult to look after my second child. What about the loss that my children will face, of each other, if Julie is adopted, let alone my loss. It wasn't my fault that she went into care. Now they are saying I am not good enough to look after my own child, even though I've been the most consistent person in her life for the past five years. She has not had the same social worker all this time. It is just a "case" to them . . .

This young mother finally lost her eight-year-old child to adoption without contact. Adopters who would accept contact could not be found and therefore the judge in the final court hearing asked for the guardian *ad litem's* opinion 'Is contact more important or is a permanent placement more important?' To this the guardian *ad litem* replied that a permanent placement was more important. It seemed that the needs of the child and the birth parent took second place to the wishes of potential adopters. The decision was not based on reasonable considerations of the full circumstances of Joanna's situation. Social services had built up a picture of this woman based on the hostile relationship that existed between them. It was not based on an understanding of her strengths and weaknesses. This mother had managed for five years to take care of her son with special needs, whilst also visiting, her daughter who was in care, on a weekly basis, and at the same time had contested the local authority's plans to have her daughter, adopted under the threat of losing contact with her completely.

The outcome of this court case is not surprising considering the adversarial process which puts social workers in a position to make recommendations about what is best for the child to the court, and appears to give the voice of the social worker greater credibility than the voice of birth parents.

Elena

A social worker from a child protection team made a referral to the project: this was a woman described as having severe learning difficulties whose five children were recently all removed from her care for reasons of neglect and inability to cope when one of the children was burned in an accident in the home. The project worker also learned that contact was supervised, because it was believed that Elena could not cope with disciplining five children, whose ages ranged from three to eleven years. The mother was not aware that assessments were being made during contact.

Through counselling it became clear that this woman did not have severe learning difficulties. She eventually learned to read and write in order to communicate with her children, with whom she was allowed monthly contact whilst they were in care. It became apparent that she was coping with many significant stresses in her life, including having recently lost her husband and mother within a month of each other.

Elena did not express overt anger and antagonism towards social services regarding the removal of her children. She was also unaware of her rights and responsibilities and asked whether social services could alter her contact arrangements at one day's notice.

This case raises issues common to many birth parents. Seen here is the problem when a system clearly discriminates in its practices against parents with learning difficulties. No specialist social workers with knowledge of learning disabilities were involved in the child protection process. Neither was there any independent advocate working with Elena to enable her to understand the maze of social work and legal processes, her rights and responsibilities whilst her children were in care, and how best to make use of her own legal advisor and to communicate with social/services.

Helen

Helen had two children removed from her because her son was sexually abused by her partner. She herself was admitted into psychiatric care as a result of a nervous breakdown. Due to her health problems, plans were being made for the children to be placed for adoption. A placement had been found in London. She fought against this, because it was too far away and it would mean she would not be able to have contact with them. Finally, it was agreed not to go for an Adoption Order and to settle the children in long-term foster care with their current carers. Supervised contact was to continue for an hour in the birth mother's house. Helen was overjoyed that her children would not be placed for adoption. However, she was unhappy that plans were not being made to rehabilitate them with her. She did not know what her rights were as a mother whose children were in the care of the local authority. She wanted to consider the possibility of her children coming home to her.

Work with Helen then revolved around exploring her own needs, her children's needs, her own personal circumstances and how she could provide for her children day-to-day on a long-term basis. Her children's welfare while with the current foster carers, the length of time they had been there, and the antagonistic relationship between the birth mother and foster carers were also discussed.

Helen decided that she was not in a position to be able to offer her children the permanent, full-time care that she so desperately wanted to give them. She decided that their needs would be better met in their foster placement, even though there had been conflict in the past and the foster carers at present did not wish to communicate with her. She said, however, that she wanted to play a significant role in her children's lives.

We looked at what this could mean in terms of where they were living. What impact did conflict between the foster carers and her have on the children? How could the conflict be resolved? What was the role of day-to-day carers of children and how would this be different from her position as a birth mother? How would the children benefit from contact with her? What level of contact could be negotiated? What was the nature of contact she hoped for and what sort of involvement did she want in their lives? What were her rights and responsibilities under the Children Act 1989?

The outcome of this work was that Helen, armed with awareness of her rights and clear about the role she wanted to play in her children's lives, met up with social services independently to begin negotiations regarding contact and resolving the conflict between herself and the foster carers.

Supporting parents in the process of contesting adoption was crucial both for birth parents and children in terms of their emotional health and adjustment. Birth parents fared better mentally knowing that they were doing all they could for their children. Children gained an understanding about why they came into care as well as knowing that they were not rejected by the important people in their lives, which is crucial for their long-term adjustment in alternative families.

The realisation that social services were not going to return the children to their care, and that the end of the road had been reached, has often been the point when mothers have individually talked about wanting to give permission to their children to settle into a new family and to let go. For example, a birth mother who was recovering from drug addiction was informed that an adoptive family had been found for her son and that she should not say anything to him about it unless he raised it during their contact visit the next day. In counselling, she expressed deep hurt because her six-year-old son had been informed by the social worker of his new family before she, the birth mother, had been told. The mother also discussed how her son must have been feeling and her pain at not being able to be with him at the time to say she loved him and that it was OK to go to his new family, who she knew would look after him well.

Social workers often fear that birth parents will make the plans for transition to an adoptive family more difficult for the children, and on this basis organise supervised access with specific instructions to birth parents not to mention the final separation. The indirect messages given to the children are that their mothers are powerless and inadequate and that mothers are not allowed to show their strength in comforting, containing and helping children to let go and look to the future. Helen is one of many parents who have made it clear that with support, parents can pursue the interests of their children first and foremost despite the pain of their loss. It is the child and mother's caring for each other that will help the transition, not the concern of the social worker to protect the child from getting hurt. It also should be acknowledged that this is a painful time for many social workers; it is important that their own feelings do not block the process of letting go.

Work with black birth parents

It is important to note that the project worker was a black woman who came from a background of community work and the refugee movement where she had provided counselling to women survivors of physical, emotional and/or sexual violence. Despite this, it was very difficult for black men and women to access the service and it seemed much harder to develop a trusting and supportive relationship with black birth parents. The issues for black birth parents being judged to be "bad" had additional implications. Their shame and guilt seemed almost greater where the decisions were made by people from a different ethnicity and culture.

Ayesha

Ayesha is a young single black woman under 25 years old. She had placed her son in voluntary care. She said:

I didn't have a clue how to look after him and on top of that he cried all the time and I wasn't getting any sleep. I just couldn't cope.

She was told by the health visitor to seek help from social services. She was also looking for alternative accommodation to get out of the bedsit she was in. She was desperate to move out of her area due to actual violence and continued threats of violence from her son's father and friends. She was isolated from her own family and had no connection with her parents. Her own life experiences included physical, sexual and emotional abuse. She had very low self-esteem and found it difficult to communicate with people. When she put her son into care, she did not know that she could lose him altogether. When she returned to get him a few months later she was informed that plans had been made for her son to be adopted.

During the time she was contesting the adoption plans, counselling covered the events leading up to the plans being made, her feelings of intense anger and loss, and her experience of discrimination. She also asked for information and help in understanding the legal and social work processes. She talked of feeling tricked by the health visitor and social worker because she had been told that social services were there to help people who were finding it difficult to cope with their child. Ayesha wanted the project worker to attend meetings with her solicitor regarding contact arrangements. The courts had decided that she could only have letter box contact, despite the fact that she had met the prospective adopters of her son. The decision was based on the anger and aggression she had shown towards social workers and other professionals.

The role of the project worker had been to listen to Ayesha's side of the story, to explore her feelings in relation to her son, her own life, her relationship with social services and to support her in negotiating contact. Once the adoption was finalised, Ayesha was unable to continue counselling for a while but got in touch again when she wanted help to set up the letter box agreement. From this point on, regular counselling was organised to deal with the impact of the adoption being finalised. She recounted:

I feel angry with social services because they did not give me a chance with my son. I know I wasn't able to take care of him. I was on my own and didn't know how to look after a baby. However, I do respect social services because of what they have given my son and that is a family. I could never have given my son a family. I feel sad and unhappy that my son can't talk to me. I have seen him talk to his adoptive parents. I am glad he can do this.

Ayesha was informed that all letters and cards she sent for her son would be read to check that they were appropriate. She asked the project worker what this meant. She discussed with the worker the card she wanted to send for her son's birthday and she enclosed a little note for the adoptive parents. She said she wanted to do this so they would know that she acknowledged them as the carers of her son and that she appreciated them for this.

Within the context of adversarial proceedings, judgments had been made that this young woman was somebody who would threaten the adoption placement if greater contact was allowed and that therefore she would have to be handled carefully by social services. Her support needs, in order to fulfill the lifelong needs of her child, were not even on the agenda; yet work with Aysha has shown her potential for change and growth.

Issues for discussion arising from the project
Birth parents or birth mothers?

Only one referral to the project came from a birth father. In all the other situations, the parent was a single woman, confirming the fact that it is usually women who are left in the position of being the main carers and, as a result, are economically dependent on either the state or a male partner. Furthermore, the majority of women's experiences contain some degree of sexual, physical and/or emotional abuse in childhood and adulthood by a male figure in their lives. There may also have been violence or sexual abuse against their children by male partners. Many women have therefore lost their children to care on the basis of their failure to protect them or because of the effect on their own mental health. More awareness is needed of the ways in which women are marginalised within society and, in particular, the findings of this project show that lack of this awareness will mean that birth mothers will lose out by not receiving appropriate support.

To take this a stage further, social work procedures must focus on the needs of these particular groups of women to enable them to care for and keep their children. This means a different starting point for social workers. So it is not about asking mothers: 'How able are you to protect your children?' The question should be: 'What do you need in order for both of us to work together to help you protect your children?'

The adversarial process recreated?

The question of whether *Before Adoption* would become an advocacy service was raised from the start of the project by various social services managers. Therefore it became urgent for the project to clarify its role in terms of advocacy and counselling. This involved discussion with representatives from social services, listening to the experiences of birth parents, and analysing the nature of requests for support. It was crucial to establish credibility and co-operation both with social services and birth parents so that the project worker could play a constructive as well as a supportive role. It was interesting to note that the discussion raised issues of power and powerlessness as well as the impact of adversarial proceedings on critical life decisions.

Social services recognised the lack of counselling provision for parents losing children to adoption and generally wanted to see *Before Adoption* provide a counselling service which, it was hoped, would enable birth parents to adjust to the loss of their children. They also, however, expressed fears that if the project offered advocacy, their work would be made much more difficult and they would have less control over their cases. Birth parents, on the other hand, were clearly requesting a combined and independent advocacy and counselling service.

Social services argued that birth parents had advocates in their solicitors who legally represented them. Also guardians *ad litem* were independent from social services and so there were safeguards built into the legal and social work systems. It was the guardian's role to examine and question the case put forward by social services. What then was the purpose of yet another advocate for birth parents? It was suggested that helping birth parents contest and challenge social work decisions and recommendations would only prolong contested proceedings which would not be in the best interests of the children in the long term. It was also suggested that it is already very difficult to work with parents who were in conflict with the local authority and this would increase the tensions between social services and birth parents rather than enable them to work co-operatively. Counselling, on the other hand, would hopefully help birth parents to relinquish their children and to work through their grief.

Before Adoption argued that advocacy and counselling were both important, not only because this was what birth parents wanted but because parents needed to be empowered to deal with their situation by questioning what was happening to them alongside exploring the emotional impact of their circumstances. This did not mean that the worker would get involved in challenging social work assessments as feared by social workers. It did, however, mean that the worker would support the birth parent in seeking clarification of information relating to social work and legal processes by helping them to understand their case and the expectations of them from social services.

Allowing an independent advocate and counsellor to work with birth parents through contested proceedings should increase the scope of "partnership" and narrow the gaps in power between the birth parents and social workers. The role of an advocate would be to help parents to put across their views to any professional involved with their case. We believed this would enable better communication between the two parties and that this would be in the long-term interests of the children.

Choices made

A research project undertaken by Barnado's found that, with adequate resourcing and support, birth families could be supported in maintaining themselves. They achieved a 78 per cent success rate in rehabilitating children with their birth families. However, the level of input had to be the same as that given to prospective adopters. Rehabilitation programmes needed a clear commitment to get the family back together as well as resources such as housing, education, benefits, childminding, residential units, support networks and social worker input to enable parents to achieve the clear aim of care order revocation.

Our work with contesting birth parents has led us to understand that the debate about advocacy is also about the power of state intervention in family life and the powerlessness experienced by birth parents, rather than partnership in crucial decision making regarding the best interests of their children. The extent of this institutional power is reinforced by research findings from *Pathways to Adoption* (Murch *et al*, 1991). It was found that Adoption Orders were granted in 95 per cent of contested cases and in 84 per cent of non-contested cases. This raises fundamental questions about whether it is really possible for social workers to provide support to contesting birth parents and whether parents and social workers can work in partnership without birth parents receiving independent and confidential counselling and advocacy. Whilst there are some very good social workers who manage to provide support to contesting birth parents, social workers should not be expected to provide this service because their authority or organisation has been involved in removing the child and is therefore almost always in conflict with the birth parents.

Clarification of advocacy

For birth parents, advocacy has meant help with negotiating contact, attendance at case conferences and meetings with solicitors, accompanying them to read social services files, as well as providing written reports for courts. There have also been expectations that a project worker's involvement in their case could change their situation.

It was therefore important to clarify the meaning of advocacy for the project. Advocacy within *Before Adoption* means assisting individuals to make informed decisions and supporting them in putting their views across to those in a more powerful position than themselves. Advocacy for birth parents, contesting the adoption of their children, was therefore seen as helping them to be informed about social work and legal processes. By the nature of the requests for advocacy from birth parents, it was clear that many did not fully understand the basic reasons for social services' involvement in their family, let alone social work and legal procedures and terminology. Many parents spoke of the emotional trauma caused by the whole process and the confusion and difficulty in understanding the jargon. A high number of birth mothers had poor reading and writing abilities, and even if parents could read and write, it was extremely painful for them to read information about their children sent through the post. The project worker assisted one birth mother with a moderate learning disability to get access to her case files and to find out the full reasons for her children being taken into care and placed for adoption against her will. When she had got in touch with the social services department herself, she had been informed that she had consented to the adoption. She was shocked. Questions need to be asked about the reason for such a basic misunderstanding and about the whole adoption process specifically in relation to parents with learning disabilities. All birth parents need to know the following:

- Why have my children been removed?
- What do social workers expect from parents in these circumstances?
- How are my children?
- What are the contact arrangements and how are they supported and negotiated?
- What social work procedures follow next, eg. panel reports, medical reports, contact plans and recommendations to the panel and the court?
- What are the roles of the different professionals, eg. guardians *ad litem*, social workers, children's solicitor, their own solicitor?
- What is a Care Order, Freeing Order and Adoption Order?
- What does openness in adoption mean and can this be negotiated?
- Legal and social work documents need to be explained in language they can understand. If parents have difficulty reading, can documents be transferred to audio tapes?

Parents also need to be given the following:
- A list of solicitors specialising in child care law (few birth parents know of the child care panel and often go to their nearest solicitors).

- Written information clearly stating that the social worker's main focus is the child and the parents come second.
- Access to minutes of relevant meetings and reports.
- An understanding of and involvement in care plans and case conferences.

Once it is clear that the adoption is going ahead, birth parents can concentrate on counselling to explore their own loss and grief and the feelings and needs of their children. However, this stage is also linked with advocacy, which can mean clarifying what level of openness is planned between the child and the family, and supporting the birth parents in negotiating this.

Clearly, given the remit of the project, a more traditional, active and challenging form of advocacy was not appropriate. When this was required, birth parents were helped to contact established organisations, such as the Family Rights Group based in London. This highlights a need for a local advocacy service for birth parents in conflict with the local authority.

The legal and social framework within which decisions are made

Social work has numerous agendas, the most powerful being that of "child protection", where there are complex multiagency procedures. Social workers are responsible for assessing the needs of the child and for accessing resources to improve the functioning of the family. When a decision is made to permanently remove a child, social workers gather evidence to prove to the court why that child should not return home. They then operate in a system where the adoption legislation is in conflict with the Children Act legislation, which stresses the importance of 'working in partnership', requiring social workers to involve families in decision-making regarding their children's future and to provide resources and support to enable that family to live together. It is therefore not surprising that even the most competent social workers find it difficult to work in partnership and to be supportive of birth parents, when such conflicting demands are made of them.

A more proactive approach is employed by social workers in France (Borthwick and Hutchinson, 1996). An interesting study was carried out in 1991 which compared the English and French child protection systems. One aspect of this study explored the ways in which partnership was achieved and discussed the differences and similarities in the roles of the French and English social workers. Whilst there were similarities in theoretical perspectives and definitions of abuse, there were differences in social work aims and practice.

The role of the French social worker is to develop a trusting relationship with the family and to become involved with the family at a far more practical level, such as having meals with them, getting to know the children and also supporting training and education. If the social worker has serious concerns regarding the family, he or she can refer the case to a judge, but the judge would have the responsibility of finding out what was happening and making his or her own assessment. The French social worker does not have the power to propose future plans for the child.

It is the judge's role to draw up plans with the parents' agreement. The children's judge meets the family informally and the family can also gain access to the judge. It would be the same judge throughout the legal process. The judge then makes decisions about the nature and extent of contact, but does not have the power to forbid all contact, nor can he or she decide on adoption. This authority lies with the higher courts. If the judge wanted to overrule parents' choices, then there would have to be very clear reasons for doing so.

The French legal system focuses on the functioning of the family and the child's welfare within it, whereas in the English system, social workers are required to show how the family has failed in caring for their children without adequate resources to improve the functioning of the family. This study underlined the informal and holistic approach to family work in the French social work and legal system, in contrast to the very powerful formal and adversarial nature of the English system.

Conclusion and recommendations

Before Adoption was set up to develop a service geared specifically to listen to the perspectives of contesting birth parents. It has been said that this could simply provide a biased picture and obscure the needs of the child. The project would argue that the current child protection system is in itself biased because it has been constructed without taking account of the experiences of those who are marginalised within society, those who are the main recipients of social services and are committed to the protection of their own children but are struggling in the face of poverty, poor housing and limited access to community resources, as well as with the impact of their own individual traumatic life events. This is not to deny the significance of child protection. Children have the least power in society and must be protected from harm whether it occurs within families or within society. However, child protection should take account of the family situation in the wider social context and seek to change it. Hence family support services and community support systems have to be developed in neighbourhoods to safeguard children as well as meet the needs of families.

Before Adoption recognises that adoption is based on major life losses for all parties of the adoption triangle and in particular for birth parents and their children. The women who used the project said that it would have been helpful to them if any agencies and individuals involved, such as social services, foster carers, prospective adopters and legal representatives had explored and negotiated open adoption arrangements for children who could not stay in their families of origin. This would require a very different approach to adoption, an approach which recognises the necessity for permanent substitute care of children but also accepts the importance of organising, supporting and maintaining openness within permanency.

There is a national need for organisations like *Before Adoption*. We have had requests for support, advice and consultancy from agencies and birth parents as far afield as Hertfordshire, the Midlands and Liverpool. Interest and demand was prompted by the Cleveland Report and the Orkney Inquiry which produced some support for birth parents as the issues of child abuse and state intervention became sensationalised through the media.

There is a place for counselling, advocacy and information services, independent from the local authority, whether birth parents are actively contesting the plans for adoption or not. Parents need help at an early stage so that there is scope for improving the chances of working in partnership with social services to obtain the best possible outcome for children, be it adoption or return to their birth families. Projects such as *Before Adoption* and *Parents without Children* need to be developed nationally, not only to provide counselling and advocacy services, but to play a significant part in informing legal and social work practice.

Today's political climate, however, is characterised by the Adoption Bill, a consultative document on services to children, which streamlines the processes in contested adoption. There is little acknowledgment of birth parents' perspectives within this document or the real issues of social inequality and limited resources that lead to scarce services for these parents.

Contesting birth parents should have the right to the information, support and counselling which would enable them to make informed decisions about the situation they find themselves in. An independent agency is in a better position to work with birth parents than a statutory service which must put the children's interests first and foremost.

The experiences, feelings and perceptions of birth parents, as revealed in the context of this project, do raise questions about how

British society deals with issues of poverty, class and disability and how social services can develop family support which is not about intervention, but about maintaining and supporting families.

Recommendations

The project recommends that:

- Social services ensure that all birth parents have an opportunity for independent support and counselling as and when they need it.
- Advocacy services are available to help birth parents understand and challenge the processes, as and when they request it.
- These services need to be easily accessible, non-stigmatising, non-judgmental, independent and confidential.
- Training programmes should be developed for social workers, guardians *ad litem*, judges, foster carers and prospective adopters, to raise awareness of the birth parents' perspective.

6 • Contesting birth mothers' group

Maureen Crank, Sue Jackson and Kinni Kansara

Introduction

As a result of the individual work done on the *Before Adoption* project, it was felt that many of the women could benefit from meeting others in similar situations. We were conscious of the extreme isolation and stigma felt by most of the women using the project. We had always planned to offer groups, but the pressure for individual work left our worker with little time.

Towards the end of the project a group was formed comprising women who already had some level of contact with the project. Most of the women invited to form the group had received counselling from the project worker. Invitations were sent to thirteen women who had expressed interest in a group and six responded saying they would like to join.

The group was to be led by the project worker and a voluntary worker from *After Adoption* who was herself a birth parent. The two group leaders met three times to get to know each other and to plan each session. The aim was for five sessions to be held on weekdays over the lunch period. This was to enable the women to fit in group meetings around their other commitments. A simple lunch was provided to help the group process along. Travel costs were reimbursed. The initial session was attended by four women, one of whom was black. The room was prepared with comfortable seats around a coffee table and scented candles in water, to give it a pleasant atmosphere. A flip-chart was used to write up what the women expected of the group and the themes they wished to cover.

It is understood that other women who expressed an interest, but did not attend, would have had difficulties making their own way into Manchester and were unable to get help to attend the group.

Aims and expectations

The overall expectations of the group were to share experiences and feelings, reduce isolation and gain support from other women who were contesting or had contested the local authority's plans for the adoption of their children. The first meeting was used to agree ground rules and how members would like the group to operate.

It was agreed that confidentiality was very important; fears were expressed of information getting back to social services. The members were reassured that group confidentiality would be respected. It was also agreed that, after the second session, the group would be closed to new members because it was essential to build up trust within the group. It was hoped to create an atmosphere that would be non-judgmental and give group members permission to express feelings as well as different views.

The group asked to cover the following areas:

1. How can we get social workers to listen to us and hear us?
2. How can we find out about our rights – we are important as well as our children.
3. In sharing our experiences can we reduce our isolation and be "normal"?
4. We need to understand why things have happened and why we feel so angry, helpless and "victims of the social services".
5. Contact issues and our role as parents from a distance.

Every week group members referred back to the initial aims and expectations and the women were happy to give each other time to discuss personal issues. When one mother had a planning meeting about her contact with her children, the group supported her both before and after the meeting by talking through what might have and what had happened.

Each session began with an update from the women about events in the previous week. The session went on to pick up on the areas the women had identified. Every woman was given an opportunity to speak and the group gave space to each one. Unlike other birth parent groups, the women did not take turns in telling their stories. It seemed that their *shame* did not allow them to do so. They did, however, use the group to talk about incidents and experiences around their losses on themes that had been identified. Anger towards partners was worked on throughout one session, though it often came up where women were still with that partner. A whole range of feelings was expressed. Shame was a predominant one.

Five women attended the group at different times but there was a core of four who attended each session.

During the last session, candles were lit for all the children of those present, including the group leaders. The mothers' hopes for these children were shared. Cards with messages of appreciation and support for each other were written and exchanged. An invitation for them to return to the agency, should they need to, was offered.

The project worker felt that, despite the fact that she was black herself, the black birth mother who attended the first sessions still felt marginalised. The project worker believes that black birth parents need an all black group.

Themes from the group

The need to share
From the first meeting, it became very clear that there was an intense desire to meet women in similar circumstances in order to reduce

isolation and to gain understanding from common experiences. Initially, members of the group asked the voluntary worker from *After Adoption* about her own experiences and feelings as a birth mother, especially in view of the fact that she had gone through over 25 years of dealing with the loss of her children. How did she feel now? Had she made contact with her children? How did she cope through the years? It seemed that the focus on the voluntary worker reflected the lifelong emotional journeys that the birth mothers in the group were confronting in their own lives. This worker's position in the group was crucial: she was seen as the checking point in terms of how they would survive this journey when the future was too frightening to even contemplate. One mother asked, 'Does it get any easier?'. The answer was: 'It is always a part of me, but over the years I am aware it became less prominent – I'll never forget, but as in bereavement, life has to go on. Certain incidents can bring feelings of loss to the forefront and anniversaries can be quite painful.' Members also compared feelings with each other: 'How do you feel when you see a baby in a pram? Do you ever feel like taking a baby?' 'I feel like there is a big hole in my stomach – completely empty – I feel like I have been torn apart, do you feel like this?'. This led to discussing the possibilities of 'our children looking for us'. Birth mothers wanted to know what this might be like. One birth mother was very forceful in saying that she was living for the day her children contacted her. It was sensitively put to her that this may not be the case, since some adoptees do not want to find their birth parents. Following this, questions were raised as to what information their children would have been given about them and what they would think of them.

It seemed that birth mothers in the group made powerful emotional connections with each other, gaining support through the realisation that they were not on their own. They shared by comforting each other, giving permission to ask and answer some very deep and painful questions about their situations and by supporting anyone in distress.

Negative feelings about social services

All the women in the group spoke of the intense anger they felt about the part social services had played in the removal of their children and in the plans to place them for adoption. Birth mothers talked of social workers betraying their trust, of social workers who did not believe what they were saying, of social workers who withheld copies of reports and information about meetings. All these things contributed to their feelings of disempowerment, injustice and frustration at not being heard.

There were different levels of acceptance of the overall duty of social services to protect children; most of the birth mothers agreed that children did need protection from abuse and that social services had a necessary part to play in this. The particular issues raised by the group were:

1. Mothers felt that their position as mothers was not acknowledged. They were concerned and worried about their children but felt their views were secondary to those of social workers. Only social services had the right to say what was good for their children and how best to protect them. This was felt to be unjust, especially in the light of knowing that even social workers have abused children.

2. Children were often moved from carer to carer, without necessarily informing the birth parent at the time. This caused a great deal of unhappiness.

3. Birth mothers were angry about limited contact arrangements. They felt that restricting contact had more to do with the fact that prospective adopters might find it difficult to cope, than with the interests of the children.

4. Having been judged as bad mothers in the eyes of social services and society, birth mothers were left with feelings of failure, low self-worth, isolation and guilt.

Backgrounds to losing children to adoption

There were some common threads in the reasons why plans were made for children to be placed for adoption. In the cases of three women, children were removed on the grounds of physical abuse and in two of these cases there was also sexual abuse by their partners. Following this, one woman had a nervous breakdown and was hospitalised for a considerable length of time. The other woman whose children were sexually abused was so intensely angry with the perpetrator that she was fearful of what her reaction might be if she ever saw him again. The third mother was struggling to confront the reality that her children had been harmed. Another birth mother had lost her children due to the physical and mental cruelty of her ex-partner and raged at him for the loss of her children and her family but was also angry with herself because she continued to have a relationship with this partner.

Final separation and contact

During one session, a birth mother described her final separation from her children. She spoke of her anguish at not being able to complete her "good-bye session". She thought she had not finished it properly as she was too distressed. The group helped her to move on and to realise the inevitability of the children being adopted. She now felt that it would ease things for her and for her children to talk to them one last time since she had not been ready before. She thought this would be settling for her children as well as for herself. She was encouraged by the group to make contact with social services and to write to her children. Questions were asked as to why social services had to struggle to hear the voice of the birth mother and could not see that birth mothers also wanted what was best for their children.

Birth parents felt that the importance of contact was not recognised. They felt that levels of contact depended entirely on how social workers perceived the situation. Mothers spoke of their contact with children after adoption being limited to photographs which they received shortly after placement. They have a need for a regular and consistent exchange of information as well as photographs. They felt social workers did not understand the precious nature of photographs of their children. This was all they had of them. One birth mother told how she had not heard about her children until the social worker wrote to ask her for some photographs of one of them, because the child had to do a project for school. The birth mother was upset when she said she had sent all she could and was afraid to let go of the remaining ones:

> *They are so precious – even to copy them is too risky, I may not get them back and they cannot be replaced.*

At the same time this birth mother did not want her son to feel that she would not let him have the photos.

All the birth mothers said that their views and emotions regarding contact were seen as insignificant, but if they felt the enormity of the loss of their children so intensely, how were the children coping?

Impact on birth mothers

All the mothers spoke of having to cope with mental and physical health problems. Strategies used to cope included alcohol abuse and remaining in dependent and violent relationships. Mothers expressed feelings of being a "bad" person and carried enormous guilt that they had let their children down.

The need to recover self-worth and to forgive themselves for their part in what had happened was explored by looking to the future and trying to be a positive resource to their children, despite not being with them.

Endings and conclusions

The group gelled very quickly. Members were able to give each other space; to listen and to hear each other; to identify with each other and to gently confront and challenge each other. This enabled the women to move on and to recognise their own strengths and abilities as well as weaknesses and to make plans to improve their lives.

The group worked intensively for five weeks and mothers felt the group had been very important and that they would not forget the experience of being part of it. They would have liked it to continue, but accepted the fact that this was not possible. They talked of keeping in touch with each other and exchanged telephone numbers and addresses. They also gave cards to each other and the leaders. On every card a special message was written from each group member and the two group leaders.

The group leaders agreed with the members that more sessions were needed but even those five sessions were of enormous value to the women: they left knowing other women who had also lost children to care and adoption. They had been able to share their tears, their laughter, anger and frustration, and they felt they had been acknowledged as mothers for life who did not do the day-to-day parenting.

The group members agreed that issues brought up in the group regarding their experiences could be recorded in a report to promote the understanding of the birth mothers' position as long as confidentiality was retained.

References

Borthwick S and Hutchinson B, *The Confidential Doctor System*, in Batty D and Cullen D (eds), *Child Protection: The therapeutic option*, BAAF, 1996.

Department of Health, *Adoption: The future*, HMSO, 1993.

Hughes B and Logan J, *Birth Parents:The hidden dimension*, University of Manchester, 1993.

Murch M, Lowe N, Borkowski M, Copner R and Griew K, *Pathways to Adoption*, Department of Health, HMSO, 1993.

Social Services Inspectorate, Department of Health, *Planning for Permanence? Adoption in three northern local authorities*, May 1993.

Trent J, *Homeward Bound – The rehabilitation of children to their birth parents*, Banardo's, 1989.

Afterword

The findings of both projects were similar in the following ways.

Contact

Birth parents who receive information and photographs were extremely grateful, but these were not in the majority, despite the fact that all of the children were past babyhood. The more adversarial the proceedings, the less contact was set up and often there was no further interest from social services. The view was that the court was still reluctant to make a Contact Order in adoption proceedings and the general negative portrayal of birth parents seemed to add to the difficulties in achieving any level of openness. Both projects also indicated that, in adoptions that were contested, there was an even lower level of contact with children post-adoption.

The Durham project highlighted the difficulties of setting up contact at the point of an adversarial court hearing, which would explain why so many contested adoptions never include any meaningful level of contact. The Manchester experience was similar.

Effects on health

Most of the birth parents involved in both projects described symptoms that indicated that their mental health had been affected by the process. They said that they had:

- dreams and nightmares;
- addiction to alcohol and drugs;
- an excessive interest in graveyards;
- anxiety/agitation;
- loss of sleep;
- depression; and
- suicidal thoughts.

The black birth parents who contacted the Manchester project mainly heard of it through their current use of mental health services.

Almost all the birth parents described relationship difficulties, fear of further pregnancy and parenting of subsequent children. Symptoms of post-traumatic stress syndrome, such as flashbacks, distressing thoughts and images and hallucinations were reported by several birth parents.

The work done on both projects gives us a better understanding of the loss and grieving process; the *Parents without Children* definition of these stages will be helpful to workers in the field:

- the need to tell the story;
- disconnectedness and anger blaming social workers – not clear about events;
- acknowledging the loss, often leading to suicidal thoughts and working through them; and
- living with the loss and learning to move on.

These stages were also clearly observed in the group facilitated by *Before Adoption*.

Conclusion

The work done on both projects demonstrated a very clear need for an independent service available nationally. Calls were regularly received by both projects from all parts of the country from birth parents and other professionals requesting help. These requests were for the following:

Information

All the birth parents in touch with both projects wanted information about adoption. This should be provided through factsheets in relevant languages and on audio cassettes. The wording should be simple and free from legal terminology and social work jargon.

Counselling and support
An independent person who can deal with the issues of loss and mourning.

Advocacy
A person who will provide support for contesting birth parents and act on their behalf.

Mediation
A person, independent of the case, who will mediate between parties to resolve the conflict in a friendly manner.

If these services were provided nationally they could be more cost effective and make it possible for birth parents to remain an ongoing resource to their children.

Many of the findings of both projects relate to present–day child-care practice. Although the Children Act 1989 promotes a philosophy of working in partnership with families, according to families involved in the projects there is little evidence of this in cases where there are child protection concerns.

There was consensus from both projects about the desperate need for family support. Lack of resources had played a large part in whether children were rehabilitated or adopted, and poverty was a common theme for most families. The recent moves to refocus resources on family support may well help to make a difference, but there is no significant shift as yet.

The last ten years saw an increasingly right wing government in the UK with an emphasis on family values and on adoption as a method of social control. There has been much talk of single parenthood and the "positive option" of adoption in these cases. The White Paper on Adoption, published in 1993, did not offer the same hope as the previous proposals. Its recommendations did not advocate significant change in adoption. *The Adoption Bill – A consultative document* tries to standardise domestic and intercountry adoption. As a result, it is unfortunate that the "good adoption practice" which we have begun to see does not feature to any great extent in the legislation. It is hard to know how, without legislation, the birth parents with whom both these projects have worked will receive services in the future. Whilst there is a lack of funding for independent agencies, local authorities will not want to put money into services, from which birth parents will be reluctant to accept help. Practice guidelines would help.

Murray Ryburn describes parents who lose their children as a result of compulsory adoption as a 'disenfranchised group' whose views are rarely heard by agencies planning for their children. He emphasises that children who are subjects of compulsory adoption are more likely to be from deprived and poor backgrounds. Certainly, both projects would support this view. Consenting birth parents were seen as more worthy than those who contested their children's adoption.

The adoption process perpetuates the disadvantage of contesting parents through lack of acknowledgment, representation and available resources. The two projects gave credence to the voice and participation of these birth parents. Both were open to the development of their services according to need, a need which is as great as those of other parties involved in adoption. To redress the balance, services like these two projects, if provided nationally, would encourage non-contesting birth parents to participate positively in planning for their children.

To end on a positive note, *After Adoption* has now set up and is developing a new service with help from Henry Smith's Charity and the Lankelly Foundation. It is a service for birth parents in the community and Styal Women's Prison, Cheshire.

Maureen Crank
Director
After Adoption

Bibliography

Allinson A J, 'Post-traumatic Stress Disorder: British Perspective', *Med Sci Law*, 31:3, 1991.

Barth R P and Berry M, *Adoption Disruption: Risks and responses*, Aldine De Guyter, 1984.

Batty D, *The Adoption Triangle*, BAAF, 1990.

Bebbington A and Miles J, 'The background of children who enter local authority care,' *The British Journal of Social Work*, 19:4, October 1989.

Beek M, 'The reality of face-to-face contact after adoption,' *Adoption & Fostering*, 18:2, 1994.

Bond T, *Standards and Ethics for Counselling in Action*, Sage, 1993.

Bornstien P E, Clayton P J, Halikas J A, Maurice W L and Robins E, 'The Depression of Widowhood after Thirteen Months', *British Journal of Psychiatry* 122: 561–6, 1973.

Bowlby J, *Attachment and Loss: Vol 2, Separation, Anxiety and Anger*, Penguin Educational, 1978.

Brodinsky D M and Schechter M D, *The Psychology of Adoption*, Oxford University Press, 1990.

Corcoran A, 'Open Adoption: the child's right,' *Adoption & Fostering*, 12:3, 1988.

DHSS, *Social Work Decisions in Childcare: Recent research findings and their implications*, HMSO, 1985.

Department of Health, *Report of Inquiry into Child Abuse in Cleveland 1987*, HMSO, 1988.

Department of Health, *Patterns and Outcomes in Child Placement – Messages from current research and their implications*, HMSO, 1991.

Department of Health, *Adoption: The future*, HMSO, 1993.

Department of Health, SSI, *Moving the Goal Posts – A study of post-adoption contact in the North East of England*, 1995.

Driver G and Miles J, *Babylon Laws*, in O'Shaughnessy T (see below).

Fahlberg V, *Helping children when they must move*, BAAF, 1981.

Goffman E, *Stigma and Social Identity*, Pelican, 1968.

Hendry A and Scourfield F, 'Unanswered Questions,' *Community Care*, 14 May 1994.

Hillias S and Cox T, *Stress in the Police Service?* Stress Research Department, 1986.

Illsley R and Thompson B, 'Women from Broken Homes,' *Sociological Review*, Vol 19, 1961.

Jordan B, 'Contested adoptions and the role of the state in family matters' in Ryburn M, *Contested Adoptions*, Arena, 1994.

Keshet H F and Rosenthal K M, 'Fathers Without Partners: A study of fathers and the family after marital separation', Totowe W J, Rowan and Littlefield, 1980.

Lambert L, 'Contested Proceedings: What research tells us', in Ryburn M, *Contested Adoptions*, Arena, 1994.

Lewis C S, *A Grief Observed*, Faber and Faber, 1961.

Lindley B, *On the receiving end: Families' experiences of the court process in care and supervision proceedings under the Children Act 1989*, FRG, 1994.

McRoy R G, 'American Experience and research on openness,' *Adoption & Fostering*, 15:4, 1991.

McWinnie A, 'Adopted Children: How they grow up' in Ryburn M, *Contested Adoptions*, Arena, 1994.

Melina L R, *Revisiting Adopted Children*, Solstice Press, 1986.

Milham S, Bullock R, Hosie K and Haak M, *Lost in Care – The problems of maintaining links between children in care and their families*, Gower, 1986.

Newell P, 'Best Interests after Cleveland,' *Adoption & Fostering*, 12:4, 1988.

O'Neil C, 'Some dilemmas of openness,' *Adoption & Fostering*, 17:4, 1993.

O'Shaughnessy T, *Adoption and Social Work and Social Theory*, Avebury, 1994.

Packman J, Randall J and Jacques W, *Who needs care? Social work decisions about children*, Blackwell, 1986.

Post Adoption Centre, London, *Groups for women who have parted with a child for adoption*, No. 2, Post Adoption Centre, 1990.

Rickford F, 'Keeping in touch,' *Community Care*, 4 April 1996.

Rockel J and Ryburn M, *Adoption Today: Change and choice in New Zealand*, Heineman/Reed, 1988, New Zealand.

Rogers C, *On Becoming a Person*, Constable, 1961.

Rogers C, *Client Centred Therapy*, Constable, 1984.

Rowe J and Lambert L, *Children who Wait*, ABAA, 1973.

Rowe J, 'Freeing for adoption: An historical perspective,' *Adoption & Fostering*, 8:2, 1984.

Rowe J, Hundleby M and Garnett L, *Child Care Now: A survey of placement patterns*, BAAF, 1989.

Ryan M, *The Children Act 1989: Putting it into Practice*, Arena, 1994.

Ryburn M, *Adoption in the 1990s: Identity and Openness*, Leamington Press, 1992.

Ryburn M, 'Contested Adoption Proceedings,' *Adoption & Fostering*, 16:4, 1992.

Ryburn M, 'Between a rock and a hard place,' *Community Care*, 11 January 1996.

Smith J A, 'Qualitative methods, identity and transitions to motherhood', *The Psychologist,* March 1995.

Sorosky A, Baran A and Pannor R, *The Adoption Triangle*, Doubleday, 1978, USA.

Sterry S and Napier H, 'From triangles to circles,' *Adoption & Fostering,* 12:3, 1988.

Teague A, 'Social Change: Social Work and the adoption of children', Gower in Ryburn M, *Contested Adoptions*, Arena 1994.

Thoburn J, 'What kind of permanence,' *Adoption & Fostering*, 9:4, 1980.

Thoburn J and Rowe J, 'A snapshot of permanent family placement,' *Adoption & Fostering*, 12:3, 1988.

Townsend P, *Poverty in the United Kingdom*, Penguin, 1979.

Triseliotis J and Hall E, 'Giving Consent to Adoption,' *Social Work Today*, 2:17, 1971.

Triseliotis J, 'Adoption with Contact,' *Adoption & Fostering*, 9:4, BAAF, 1985.

Triseliotis J, 'Some moral and practical issues in adoption work', *Adoption & Fostering*, 13:2, 1989.

Triseliotis J, 'Evolution or revolution?' *Adoption & Fostering*, 19:2, 1995.

Walby C, 'The Adoption Law Review: policy and resource implications', *Adoption & Fostering*, 19:1, 1995.

Wallerstein J S, 'The long-term effects of divorce on children: A review, in *Journal of American Academy of Child Adolescents Psychiatry* 30:3, May 1991, USA.